green press
INITIATIVE

Nomad Press is committed to preserving ancient forests and natural resources. We elected to print *Discover the Desert: The Driest Place on Earth* on 4,315 lb. of Rolland Enviro100 Print instead of virgin fibres paper. This reduces an ecological footprint of:

Tree(s): 37
Solid waste: 1,057kg
Water: 100,004L
Suspended particles in the water: 6.7kg
Air emissions: 2,321kg
Natural gas: 151m3

It's the equivalent of:
Tree(s): 0.8 American football field(s)
Water: a shower of 4.6 day(s)
Air emissions: emissions of 0.5 car(s) per year

Nomad Press made this paper choice because our printer, Transcontinental, is a member of Green Press Initiative, a nonprofit program dedicated to supporting authors, publishers, and suppliers in their efforts to reduce their use of fiber obtained from endangered forests.

For more information, visit www.greenpressinitiative.org

FSC
Mixed Sources
Product group from well-managed forests, controlled sources and recycled wood or fibre

Cert no. SW-COC-000952
www.fsc.org
© 1996 Forest Stewardship Council

OTHER TITLES IN THE DISCOVER YOUR WORLD SERIES

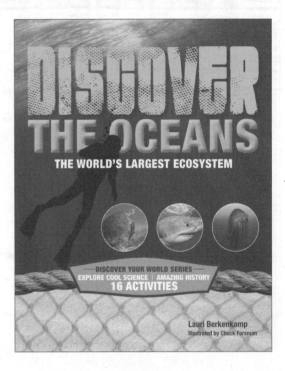

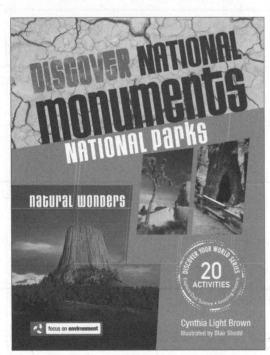

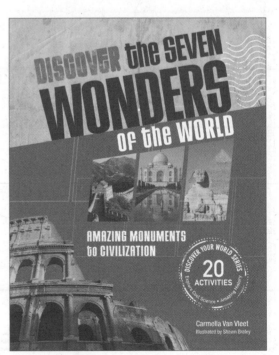

DISCOVER
THE DESERT

THE DRIEST PLACE ON EARTH

—DISCOVER YOUR WORLD SERIES—
EXPLORE COOL SCIENCE | AMAZING HISTORY
20 ACTIVITIES

Kathy Ceceri

Illustrated by Samuel Carbaugh

Nomad Press
A division of Nomad Communications
10 9 8 7 6 5 4 3 2 1
Copyright © 2009 by Nomad Press

This book was manufactured by Transcontinental, Gagné
Louiseville Québec, Canada

October 2009, Job #36495
ISBN: 978-1-9346704-6-0

Illustrations by Samuel Carbaugh

Questions regarding the ordering of this book should be addressed to
Independent Publishers Group
814 N. Franklin St.
Chicago, IL 60610
www.ipgbook.com

Nomad Press
2456 Christian St.
White River Junction, VT 05001

CONTENTS

Erg Desert Formation in Algeria

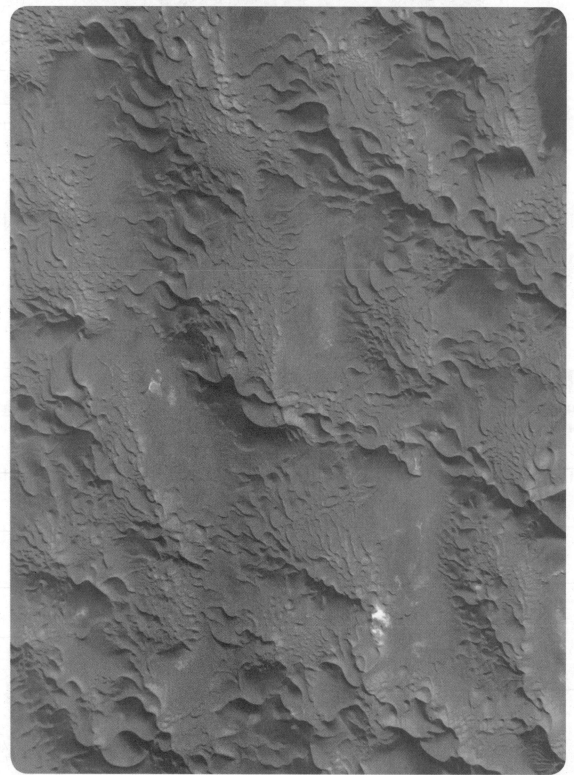

Image courtesy of the
Image Science & Analysis Laboratory, NASA Johnson Space Center

INTRODUCTION

The Driest Place on Earth

At first glance, the desert looks vast, bleak, and empty. The sun beats down, baking the ground until it's dry and parched. Dust and sand blow in your eyes, hair, and clothes. The few trees and plants provide little shade. There are no buildings, no roads. If any animals are around, they must be hiding underground. Why on Earth would you want to visit such a place?

Because there's a lot more to the desert than heat, sun, and sand. In fact, it's a world of unique sights and experiences waiting to be discovered.

Wish You Were Here!

1

The desert offers dramatic landscapes filled with enormous sand dunes, twisting canyons, and lonely outcroppings of weathered stone. It's also home to many sacred sites of ancient civilizations. And the hidden riches in the desert are more than just legend. A third of the world's diamonds and gold can be found here, and half of the world's oil!

The desert draws teams of scientists looking for fossils, meteors, and lost civilizations. Biologists come to study some of the world's most unusual plants and animals. And athletes and adventurers travel there for thrilling sports like river rafting and sand boarding.

Ready to start your desert journey? Great! This book is full of fun facts and useful information that will help you find your way around deserts all over the world. Here's a taste of what you'll discover in the chapters ahead:

- **What Is a Desert?** talks about the different types of deserts (they're not all hot!), where they're located, how they're formed, and why they're important to the rest of the planet.
- **Planning Your Desert Expedition** reveals some of the unique plants and animals that live in the desert, as well as natural formations and man-made landmarks.
- **Getting Around in the Desert** covers various ways to travel, from the most ancient to the most modern.
- The next chapters provide information on how to stay safe and healthy in the desert's harsh environment. **Water, the Most Important Resource** is a look at how desert-dwellers find water in some of the driest regions on the planet. But **Clothing, Shelter, and Food** are also vital to desert survival. Here you'll learn about old and new techniques for remaining comfortable in conditions that can range from mildly unpleasant to extreme.

- Even the best-equipped travelers need to be aware of **Desert Dangers and How to Avoid Them**. Learn how to find your way and how to deal with threats, both natural and man-made.
- And though the desert is rough, it's very fragile too. We'll conclude by looking at why we must treat the desert with respect if we want to keep the planet in balance.

To make your journey even more exciting, throughout this book you'll see invitations to **Try This**. These are ideas for science, history, and art projects designed to teach you more about the desert and even make you feel like you're there (even if you're not!). Be sure to check out the resources at the back of the book for ways to learn more. But now it's time to turn the page and begin to *Discover the Desert*.

NOTE

Some of the activities need a hot, sunny spot. If it's not hot and sunny where you are, try using a desk lamp with a warm light bulb to provide the needed heat and light. Be careful not to get the light bulb close enough to start a fire and make sure you have adult supervision.

CHAPTER 1

What Is a Desert?

There are many ways to describe a **desert**. According to the dictionary, a desert is a place that gets less than 10 inches (25 centimeters) of rain a year. That's not a lot of water if you're a plant or animal looking for a drink. A desert can also be considered a **biome** made up of organisms that have adapted to long periods of **drought**. Still another way to identify a desert is as an **arid** region with few plants and large patches of bare surface.

Each of these definitions looks at deserts differently, but all point to the same regions of the globe. Exactly how dry is a desert compared to other types of **climate**? Well, the average amount of **precipitation** in the United States (not including Alaska and Hawaii) is 30 inches (75 centimeters) a year.

—FASCINATING FACT—
Some deserts get more than 10 inches of precipitation a year—and lose almost all of it to **evaporation** and **transpiration**.

WORDS TO KNOW

desert: a place that gets less than 10 inches of rain a year.

biome: a large natural area with a distinctive climate, geology, water resources, and plants and animals that are adapted for life there.

drought: a long period of dry weather that affects living things in the environment.

arid: extremely dry.

climate: the long-term average weather pattern of a region.

precipitation: all forms of wet weather, including rain, snow, sleet, and hail.

evaporation: when liquid water is converted into vapor by the sun or other heat source.

transpiration: when a plant loses water vapor through the openings in its leaves or stem.

Wet, green states like New York, Georgia, or Washington may receive about 40 or 50 inches (100 to 125 centimeters). In other words, those states can get more rain in a month than arid Nevada gets in an entire year.

There are some deserts where it may not rain for years. A place called Bagdad in California holds the record for the longest dry streak in United States history—767 days without rain. But that's nothing. A city called Arica in Chile has gone 14 years without a drop. And some parts of Chile's Atacama Desert may see a century go by between showers!

All deserts are dry, but they can be different in other ways. Scientists categorize deserts using a variety of systems. Some systems sort them by temperature. Others sort them by geology, or what they're made of. Still others group deserts according to where they're located.

---**FASCINATING FACT**---

The driest place in the United States is Death Valley, California. It averages less than 2 inches (5 centimeters) of rain a year. Meanwhile, the wettest place in the United States is Mt. Waialeaie in Hawaii. It gets an average of about 400 inches (1,016 centimeters) of rain a year! That's an astonishing 33 feet (10 meters) of precipitation!

Kyzyl-Kum Desert

Iranian Desert

Gobi Desert

Arabian Desert

Kura Kura Desert

Taklamakan Desert

Great Basin Colorado Desert

Mojave

Sonoran

Chihuahuan Desert

Sahara Desert

Thar Desert

Patagonian Desert

Great Sandy Desert

Atacama Desert

Namib Desert

Gibson Desert

Great Victoria

Kalahari Desert

TYPES OF DESERTS BY CLIMATE

The hottest places on Earth are deserts, but only about half of all deserts are hot. Some are cool, and some are even cold!

Hot Deserts: The largest and most famous hot desert in the world is the Sahara in northern Africa. It covers 3.5 million square miles (9 million square kilometers). Other hot deserts include the Sahara's neighbor, the Arabian Desert, as well as the Great Western Desert in Australia (which includes the Great Sandy and Gibson Deserts), the Namib and the Kalahari in southern Africa, the Sonoran Desert in the southwestern United States, and the Thar on the borders of India and Pakistan. Temperatures in these hot deserts can reach 130 degrees Fahrenheit (55 degrees Celsius) and higher.

Cold Deserts: Cold deserts make up about a quarter of all deserts. In the summer, they may hit broiling temperatures like their hot cousins. But in the winter, temperatures can go down to well below freezing. It's not uncommon to see snow in the Gobi Desert of Mongolia, which is nearly a mile above sea level. Argentina's Patagonian desert is much lower in **elevation**, but its location near the Antarctic Circle gives it chilly winters as well.

Cool Deserts: Then there are the cool deserts, which include parts of the Namib in southern Africa and the Atacama in Chile.

The sections of these deserts that lie along the coast are cooled by ocean currents. For months on end, the only moisture these deserts see is dew and fog. But the temperatures are pretty steady and comfortable. In summer the average temperature is between 55 and 75 degrees Fahrenheit (13–24 degrees Celsius), and in winter the thermometer drops to about 40 degrees Fahrenheit (4 degrees Celsius).

WORDS TO KNOW

elevation: distance above or below sea level.

humidity: the amount of water vapor present in the air.

Western Hemisphere: the half of the earth that includes North and South America.

Why Is the Desert So Hot?

If there's any moisture in the soil or the air, some of the sun's heat and energy will go to evaporating it. That's why temperatures in the damp, humid rainforest rarely get above 90 degrees Fahrenheit (32 degrees Celsius). But in the desert the soil is dry and the **humidity** is close to zero. That means almost all the sun's warmth ends up heating the air and the ground, sending temperatures soaring to 120 degrees Fahrenheit (49 degrees Celsius) and above.

Another reason deserts are so hot is because many of them actually sit *below* sea level. The lower you go the hotter it gets. Every 1,000 feet (305 meters) you go up or down can mean a difference of about 5.5 degrees Fahrenheit (9.8 degrees Celsius per kilometer). For example, Dakol, Ethiopia, lies at 375 feet (114 meters) below sea level. It boasts the world's highest average temperature of 94 degrees Fahrenheit (34.5 degrees Celsius). The lowest point in the **Western Hemisphere** is Death Valley, California. At 267 feet (81 meters) below sea level, it can reach temperatures as high as 134 degrees Fahrenheit (57 degrees Celsius).

TYPES OF DESERTS BY TERRAIN

Sand **dunes** may be the first thing you think of when you picture the desert. But only about 20 to 30 percent of desert terrain is covered with sand. Let's look at different types of desert terrain.

Barchan

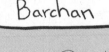

Sandy Deserts: A large, flat area of sandy desert is called an **erg**. Only a quarter of the great Sahara desert is erg, while the Great Sandy Desert in Australia is nearly all erg. The Southern Namib Erg in Africa boasts the tallest dunes in the world—they're nearly 1,000 feet (300 meters) high!

Sand dunes are formed when the wind picks up grains of sand and makes them hop along in a movement called **saltation**. Dunes come in different shapes and patterns, depending on the **prevailing wind**, the kind of plants in the area, and the size, shape, and make-up of the grains of sand themselves.

Parabolic

WORDS TO KNOW

dune: a hill or ridge of sand piled up by the wind.
erg: Arabic for sea of sand.
saltation: jumping.
prevailing wind: wind that blows mostly from one direction.

Linear

* **Barchan dunes** are crescent-shaped. Their arms point forward as they are pushed along by the wind.

* **Parabolic dunes** are also crescent-shaped, but they face backwards. They form because plants grow on their arms, holding them in place as the dunes are pushed forward by the wind.

* **Linear dunes** are straight or slightly wavy, and can form in areas with thin layers of sand or when a parabolic dune splits apart into two separate lines.

Star

* **Star dunes** get their tell-tale shape from winds that keep changing direction.

TRY THIS: create a sand Design Bottle

In marketplaces in the Middle East, craftsmen sell sand design bottles as souvenirs for tourists. Search for "sand bottle" videos on YouTube. Then watch how people use different colored sands and long narrow funnels to make their designs. Now make one of your own!

SUPPLIES

- newspaper or cut-open recycled bags to cover work space
- colored sand or regular sand and various colors of sidewalk chalk
- narrow clear recycled jar with a top (remove the label)
- one paper plate for each color of sand or make "trays" with scrap paper
- scrap paper to make funnel
- tape
- pencil, skewer, or other thin stick

3 Make a long, narrow funnel by rolling up the scrap paper. Roll tightly at one corner and gradually let the other end open up. When done, the large end should be about 1 inch (2.5 centimeters) across. Tape the funnel so it holds its shape.

4 Scoop up some colored sand with the large end of the funnel. Point the smaller end into the jar and let the sand pour out until it comes a little way up the side. Keep adding layers of different colors. Use the small end of the funnel to point the sand where you want it to go. Don't worry what color goes in the center of the jar. The only sand that will show is what's up against the inside of the glass.

1 Cover your work area. If you are using sand from the beach or your backyard, rinse it first and let it dry. Sift out any large particles.

2 To color your sand, pour a small amount onto a paper plate. Roll a piece of sidewalk chalk over the sand until the color is dark enough. Make several colors in this way. If you are using colored sand, pour some of each color on a separate plate.

5 You can use the stick to poke through the different layers and make dips and ridges. Continue adding sand until the bottle is full. Seal the jar tightly.

Rocky Deserts: In some places like the southwestern United States, deserts are filled with flat-topped hills and mountains called **plateaus**. These plateaus consist of layers of rock laid down over millions of years. The layers may have started out as soft mud or sand carried by oceans or rivers that once covered the area.

In other places **molten** volcanic material may have flowed over the surface, or minerals in the ground water may have seeped in and combined with the layers already there. Ancient plants and animals of the time were often trapped in the soft layers. And as more layers piled on top, the weight compressed the soft material into hard stone. Today those layers can be seen in **canyons** where **erosion** caused by water, wind, or heating and cooling have opened cracks in the rock and worn down the rocky plateaus.

Rocky deserts also feature broad flat plains covered with loose pebbles or gravel. These plains have different names depending on where you are. They're called **desert pavement** in the United States, **reg** in the Middle East, **gibber** in Australia, and **gobi** in China.

Some of these plains have shallow lakes, many of which are salty. The most famous of these are the Great Salt Lake in Utah and the Dead Sea bordering Israel and Jordan in the Middle East. Sometimes these lakes dry up. The cracked, muddy clay beds they leave behind are called **playas**.

—FASCINATING FACT—

Many sources report that the name of China's largest desert, the Taklamakan, means "you go in but you don't come out." But in 2005 a Chinese researcher studying the language of the local Uighar people in the region disagreed. He said the name actually comes from the Turkish word "takli," which means "poplar tree." The meaning of the name is still being argued—but it is true that 1,500 years ago poplars grew where there is now just bare desert.

WORDS TO KNOW

plateau: a flat, high area.

molten: made liquid by heat.

canyon: a deep, narrow valley with steep sides carved by flowing water.

erosion: being worn away by wind or water.

desert pavement, reg, gibber, gobi: a thin surface layer of closely packed pebbles.

playa: a dry lake bed with a hard, flat, clay bottom.

Giant Sequoia Cactus

10

TYPES OF DESERT BY LOCATION

Mellon Cactus

Winds can carry moisture from the ocean onto land. But when dry winds blow across land, they can carry any moisture away, creating a desert. Certain places on Earth are more likely to have dry air currents than others. These locations are where the world's deserts are found.

Subtropical Deserts: Many deserts are found in the **subtropics**. These are two bands around the earth, to the north and the south of the **tropics** along the equator. Subtropical deserts are caused by air currents called **Hadley Cells**. These currents draw hot moist air up from the ocean over the equator. Then they drop the moisture as rain over the tropics, creating tropical rainforests. The air that falls back to Earth in the subtropics has no moisture left. This dry air flows back to the equator, heats up, and begins the cycle again. Subtropical deserts include the Sahara, Sonoran, and Thar in the north, and the Kalahari and Great Western deserts in the south.

Continental Deserts: Some parts of the earth are dry partly because they're in the middle of continents. This is because ocean breezes, full of water vapor, release their moisture as rain or other precipitation once they hit land. The farther air has to travel over land, the dryer it gets. Continental deserts include the Monte in South America, the central deserts of Australia, the Great Basin and Chihuahuan deserts in North America, and China's Taklamakan and Gobi deserts.

WORDS TO KNOW

subtropics: the region of the earth to the north and south of the tropics.

tropics: the region of the earth around the equator.

Hadley cell: currents of air moving over the subtropic and tropic zones.

radiate: send out energy.

From Hot to Cold and Back Again

Don't be fooled by the name—hot deserts get cold too! At night under clear skies, the heat of the desert **radiates** into the atmosphere from both the ground and the air. In Death Valley, California, the record low temperature is zero degrees Fahrenheit (-18 degrees Celsius). In the Sonoran Desert of Arizona in the wintertime, the temperature can drop 50 degrees at night.

---FASCINATING FACT---

The polar desert of the Antarctic Dry Valleys was once thought to be sterile and lifeless. But now the valleys are known to be home to several primitive but important forms of life such as moss, algae, bacteria, and tiny roundworms called nematodes. Scientists believe the nematodes may play a vital role in preventing **carbon dioxide** from being released into the air, where it contributes to **global warming**.

Rain Shadow Deserts: Land on the far side of a mountain range can end up as a rain shadow desert. This happens when moist ocean breezes hit a mountain range. To get over the mountains, the breezes must blow upward. As they go up they get colder, which means they can't hold as much water vapor. The moisture is released as precipitation on the mountain, and the dry air continues on its way. Rain shadow deserts include the Patagonian Desert in South America (which is blocked by the Andes), the Great Basin to the east of Oregon's Cascade Mountains, and the deserts of Central Asia (which are downwind of the Himalayas).

Rain Shadow Deserts

Coastal Deserts: Along some parts of the western edge of Africa and the Americas, cold water currents flow along the coast. The cold ocean air can't hold much moisture, so dry winds blow onto the shore. This creates a coastal desert. Coastal deserts get most of their moisture in the form of fog. Examples include the Atacama Desert in Chile, the Namib in southern Africa and Baja California in Mexico.

WORDS TO KNOW

carbon dioxide: a gas that can trap the sun's heat in the air. It is produced by breathing, by rotting dead matter, and by burning fossil fuels like oil and coal.

global warming: climate change that causes the average temperature of the air and oceans to rise.

wadi, arroyo: dry channel cut by water.

yardang: a ridge of rock shaped by wind.

Polar Deserts: Polar deserts are found near the North and South Poles, where the air is too cold to hold any moisture and the surface water is frozen for much of the year. As with other deserts, there is little precipitation. On the continent of Antarctica at the South Pole, precipitation (in the form of ice and snow, of course) is equal to about 2 to 8 inches (5 to 20 centimeters) of rain per year. Although some areas have snow dunes, many parts, like the McMurdo Dry Valleys, are made up of bare rock. Near the North Pole, parts of Greenland, Russia, Scandinavia, and northern Alaska are considered polar deserts.

HOW ARE DESERTS SHAPED?

Rainbow Bridge

Water erosion: Water, in the form of heavy rains and floods, plays a big role in shaping the desert. With so little soil and plant life to absorb the water, most rain flows off quickly, forming channels in the sand or filling empty river beds. These beds are called **wadis** in the Middle East and **arroyos** in the Americas.

Small bits of rock and sand carried by the fast-flowing streams can wear away at the surrounding stone. This water erosion sometimes produces interesting or unusual shapes. The pink sandstone Rainbow Bridge in Utah was carved out of rock by a river millions of years ago.

Wind erosion: The other major force shaping the desert is wind. Given enough time, small grains of sand blown by the wind can widen cracks in a plateau until smaller mesas and solitary buttes are formed. Wind also creates desert pavement by blowing away smaller dirt particles to reveal a thin surface layer of closely packed pebbles.

Salt crystallization: Many desert areas have lots of salt in the soil and groundwater. When salt crystals begin to form in the cracks and crevices of rocks, it can push them apart. Salt washed into the canyons by heavy rains also accumulates on desert floors. These can become enormous, smooth salt flats.

TRY THIS: grow salt crystals

The Bonneville Salt Flats in Utah and many other desert areas are covered in salt crystals formed by the evaporation of salt water. Here's a quick and easy way to create your own salt crystals at home.

SUPPLIES

- microwave-safe bowl
- 1 cup water
- microwave
- about ¹/₂ cup salt
- shallow dish
- small piece of absorbent cardboard
- dry plate

1 Heat the water in the microwave for 3 minutes. Remove carefully! Ask a grown-up for help. Stir in the salt until no more will dissolve and it begins piling up on the bottom of the bowl. Carefully pour just the water into the shallow dish.

2 Lay the piece of cardboard in the water. Let it soak through. Remove the cardboard and place it on the dry plate. Salt crystals will start to form immediately.

WHY ARE THE DESERTS IMPORTANT?

Only about 8 percent of the world's population lives in or near deserts. But deserts have many important ties to the rest of the planet. Besides being home to all kinds of unique wildlife, deserts serve as a resting place for non-desert species migrating across them, such as storks from Europe. Desert sands contain micro-organisms that store carbon dioxide and may help to keep it from adding to global warming.

—FASCINATING FACT—

A desert rose or sand rose is a rock crystal that looks remarkably like a flower. It's found in deserts around the world where underground salt water levels go up and down during the seasons. In Saudi Arabia near the Arabian Gulf, it's easy to find desert roses within arm's reach under the sand.

And desert dust storms fertilize oceans and tropical areas thousands of miles away by depositing iron and other minerals.

In past eras deserts were heavily used as trade routes for goods and cultures. Today deserts are a major source of fossil fuels, such as oil, and other valuable minerals, including gold, diamonds, and uranium. Some scientists are even working on ways to turn deserts into much-needed farmland. Others want to use the bright sunlight and windswept open spaces of deserts to produce clean energy from wind and solar power.

— FASCINATING FACT —

A **yardang** is a ridge of rock shaped by the blowing of desert winds. Egypt's famous Sphinx was probably carved out of an existing yardang.

But for now, the desert is an exciting place to visit and explore. Before you set out on your expedition, however, it's a good idea to make a list of what there is to see and do in the desert.

How Can the Desert Wind Move Rocks?

Sure, the wind is mighty enough to move a sand dune—grain by grain. But can it move rocks weighing hundreds of pounds? Amazingly, that's the theory behind the sliding rocks in Death Valley National Park in California.

In the park there's a playa known as the Racetrack, about 2 miles (3 kilometers) long and 1 mile (1.6 kilometers) wide. On it you can see long, winding skid marks left by the rocks as they wandered across the flat mud floor. There are no footprints to suggest that something or someone gave the rocks a nudge. No one has ever seen the rocks move. Some tracks stretch for 1,500 feet (458 meters).

Scientists believe that when it rains, the hard, cracked playa floor turns into a layer of slick wet clay. This makes it possible for winds up to 50 miles (80 kilometers) an hour to push the boulders across the slippery surface. But until someone catches them in the act, the sliding rocks of Death Valley will remain a mystery.

TRY THIS: make a desert rock layer pendant

The Grand Canyon in Arizona is a channel cut through desert rock by the Colorado River. It is 300 miles (450 kilometers) long, up to 6,000 feet (1,800 meters) deep, and began forming 5–6 million years ago. When you look at the canyon walls, you can see layers of limestone, sandstone, shale, and other rock that were stacked up between 1,800 million and 270 million years ago. The different layers make up a brilliant landscape of pink, yellow, orange, red, brown, and black stripes. With colored polymer clay, you can make your own desert rock layer pendant to wear around your neck.

1 Look at some images of the Grand Canyon's layers as a guide. Starting with blue for the water of the river, make a thin layer of clay about 2 inches (5 centimeters) square. Make another thin layer of another color on top, a little smaller than the first.

2 Keep adding layers, each a little smaller, until your "canyon" is as high as you would like your pendant to be. Press the layers so that they stick together.

3 Squeeze the stack of layers slightly for a natural look. With the toothpick, draw lines running down for water channels. For wider channels, carve some "rock" away with your knife.

echo!

Kaibab Limestone
Toroweap Formation
Coconino Sandstone
Hermit Shale
Supat Group
Redwall Limestone
Bright Angel Shale
Tapeats Sandstone
Vishnu Schist
Zoraster Graphite

echo!

4 Carefully slice through all the layers to make a multi-layered sliver about ¼-inch (½-centimeter) wide. Use the toothpick to make a hole in the pendant large enough to fit the cord through.

5 Bake according to package directions. Let cool, then cut a piece of cord long enough to fit around your neck and thread it through the hole. Knot it just above the pendant. Tie the ends together.

CHAPTER 2

Planning Your Desert Expedition

he desert has always attracted people ready for adventure and new experiences. There are many unusual desert landforms and creatures that can't be found anywhere else on Earth. Some of the earliest civilizations got their start in the desert, leaving behind mysteries that scientists still can't explain. And new technologies are making it possible for people to do things in the desert never before possible. Let's take a closer look at what the desert has to offer!

NATURE'S ODDITIES AND SPLENDORS

Desert plants and animals sometimes look like they belong on another planet. This is because they're designed for getting and holding water, or getting along without water. In a land where it may not rain for months or years, making the most of the moisture you've got is the key to a happy life.

Desert life forms are divided into three categories depending on their survival tactics. "Drought resistors" have special adaptations

that keep them from drying out. For example, animals may seek out shade or burrow into the mud during the day. Plants like the cactus, a type of **succulent**, may have small, spiny leaves and sunken pores that reduce evaporation. Some plants store water in their spongy trunks, stems, or roots. Other plants, like the yucca, send down large tap roots deep underground to seek out water.

"Drought tolerators" can almost completely dry up and still survive. For example, the triops, a type of **crustacean** dating back to the time of the dinosaurs, lays egg-like cysts that can wait months or years in the parched soil until the next storm. The seeds of most desert wildflowers lie dormant until a good drenching

WORDS TO KNOW

succulent: a type of plant with spongy tissue that holds moisture.
crustacean: an aquatic animal like a shrimp or crab with a hard outer shell.

TRY THIS: Hatch Your Own Pet Triops

The entire lifespan of a triops, also known as a tadpole shrimp, is only one to three months. But they grow at an enormous rate until they reach about 2 inches (5 centimeters) in length. They're easy to raise and fun to observe.

1 Put a thin layer of sand on the bottom of your container. Add water according to the kit's directions.

2 Place the thermometer on the foil. The temperature should be 73–85 degrees Fahrenheit (23–30 degrees Celsius). If it is too cool, place a lamp so it shines on the container. Cover one end of the container with aluminum foil for shade.

3 Add the nutrient and eggs according to the kit's directions. Within a day you should see miniscule triops swimming around. After a week you can feed them bits of carrot and brine shrimp in addition to food pellets.

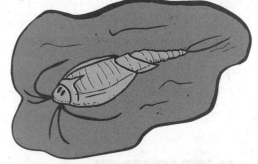

Supplies

- clean sand (rinse with bottled water)
- clear container, such as a plastic take-out clamshell box (rinse with bottled water)
- 1–2 gallons (4–8 liters) bottled or non-chlorinated water
- triops kit with eggs, nutrients, and food pellets (available at toy stores or www.triops.com)
- small thermometer
- aluminum foil
- warm spot or desk lamp
- bits of carrot and brine shrimp

signals them to spring into action. There are also plants like moss that can go completely dry and green up again over and over.

"Drought avoiders" live only in areas where there is enough water to survive. Animals migrate to greener areas. Plants like columbine flowers in the southwestern U.S. and date palms in the Middle East thrive only around rivers or pools where their roots can reach underground water easily.

WEIRD DESERT PLANTS

The cactus is a type of plant that was originally found only in the deserts of North and South America. (One variety was also found in Africa, Sri Lanka, and Madagascar.) And it's different from other plants in several ways. A cactus usually has a spongy trunk or stem for storing water. It has few, if any, branches. Its green trunk has **chlorophyll** and **stomata** that take the place of leaves for making food by **photosynthesis**. And it's got spines—long, thin needles that often grow in clusters along the trunk and can really hurt if you brush against them.

The saguaro (pronounced sah-wah-roh) cactus of the Sonoran Desert in Arizona sometimes resembles a green telephone pole with arms bent upward at the elbow. It takes 50–70 years for the saguaro to grow its first branch! Luckily, its life span can reach 200 years. The saguaro stores water in its expandable trunk, which has ribs that spread like an accordion as it fills. The ribs slowly collapse again as the stored water is used up. Saguaros can top 50 feet (15 meters) in height and weigh over 6 tons.

WORDS TO KNOW

chlorophyll: a green coloring found in plants, which helps absorb light energy for photosynthesis.

stomata: a tiny pore in a plant that can be opened or closed to let air pass through.

photosynthesis: a process in plants in which carbon dioxide gas from the air combines with water and light energy to make sugars. The sugars are used by plants for food.

The Joshua tree, found mainly in the Mojave Desert in California, has been called "the most repulsive tree in the vegetable kingdom." This member of the yucca family has shaggy bark and thick branches that end in spiky green leaf blades. It can grow to be 80 feet (24 meters) tall and 12 feet (3.6 meters) around. One tree in Joshua Tree National Park in California is believed to be nearly 900 years old!

TRY THIS: Plant a Cactus Dish Garden

A cactus dish garden is easy to set up and needs very little care. Just keep an eye on it to see when the plants are starting to look a little shrunken and limp, then give them a moderate watering. Your garden may only need to be watered once every few weeks or months.

1 If there is a hole in the bottom of your pot, cover it with a stone or piece of broken pot. Then cover the bottom of the pot or bowl with a layer of small pebbles for drainage.

2 Fill the pot almost to the top with cactus potting soil or a mixture of half sand, half regular potting soil. Pile the soil higher in the middle so it slopes down to the sides of the bowl.

3 Insert the plants by using the spoon to dig a hole for each plant's roots. Put taller plants in the center and shorter plants around the edge. Be sure to leave some room to grow around each plant.

4 Cover the soil with a layer of sand. Add rocks or other decorations, or create a "dry river bed" with pebbles.

Sand

WEIRD DESERT ANIMALS

In hot deserts, animals have developed interesting ways of moving so they don't touch the scorching surface too much. For example, the sidewinder snake travels in stages. First, it throws its head to the side. Then, it flips a coil of its belly after it. Finally, it snaps its tail along behind. Its trail looks like a series of unconnected "S" shapes in the sand.

Sidewinder Snake

Fennec Fox

The kangaroo rat, like its namesake, hops across the sand on its hind feet. The desert iguana is a lizard that folds up its front legs and scoots across the scorching ground like a beachgoer who forgot his flip-flops. And just like in the cartoons, the bird known as the roadrunner flattens out its head and tail even with the ground as it runs up to 18 miles (29 kilometers) an hour.

Some animals have body shapes that help them keep cool. The fennec fox and the jackrabbit both sport ridiculously outsized ears sticking up out of their heads. Their ears are thin, almost transparent, and filled with blood vessels that allow some of the body's heat to radiate away into the atmosphere.

WORDS TO KNOW

clone: an organism that is genetically identical to its parent.

Ice Age: a period of time in Earth's history (that ended about 10,000 years ago) when a large portion of the planet's surface was covered by ice.

The Oldest Plant in the World

Scientists believe that the King Clone creosote bush ring in the Mojave Desert is nearly 12,000 years old. A creosote bush consists of long branches growing out of a circular stem crown. As the crown expands, the inner branches die off and new branches spring up around the edge. After 30 to 90 years, clumps of new branches form their own individual plants—each an exact **clone** of the original. The King Clone ring is 45 feet (14 meters) across and has probably been around since the last **Ice Age**.

Meanwhile, the African ostrich has thick feathers on top to insulate it from the sun. Its thinly covered belly releases heat. This bird weighs 200–300 pounds (90–130 kilograms) and can't fly, but it can run almost 50 miles (80 kilometers) an hour for 30 minutes at a time.

Other animals have shapes that help them retain water. For instance, the thorny devil is an Australian reptile covered head to toe in pointy bumps. It can slurp the dew that falls on its back using grooves that act like gutters.

And of course there's the camel, which is so strange looking that it's been called "a horse designed by a committee." Dromedaries of the Middle East have one hump while Bactrian camels in China and Mongolia have two. Both kinds of humps store fat, not water. But camels can drink up to 30 gallons (114 liters) at a time. They're famous for going a week or more without water, and several months without food.

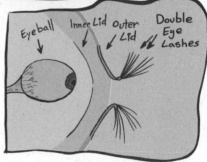

Jackrabbit

FASCINATING FACT

To protect its face from sandstorms, the camel has clear inner eyelids, double rows of extra-long eyelashes, and nostrils that close. Its huge splayed feet act just like snowshoes, spreading the camel's weight across a wide area to keep it aloft in the soft desert sand.

Eyeball   Inner Lid   Outer Lid   Double Eye Lashes

Camel Eye Diagram

DESERT MICROORGANISMS

There is life even in areas of the desert where nothing seems to grow. These microscopic creatures may be too small for you to see with the naked eye, but they are vitally important to the health of the desert—and the planet.

WORDS TO KNOW

lichen: a combination of fungus and algae.
algae: a small, plant-like organism.

Biological soil crusts are communities of microorganisms. Made up of bacteria, **lichens**, mosses, and **algae**, they blanket open soil where plants don't grow.

23

These crusts can take between 20 and 250 years to become thick enough to notice. But in some dry regions, they make up more than 70 percent of the living ground cover.

Biological soil crusts are important because they absorb water and hold together soil that would otherwise blow away. This supports other plant life. It cuts down on dust in the atmosphere, which can end up as air pollution half a world away. Soil crusts also take in and give off large amounts of carbon dioxide. This plays a part in global warming that scientists are still working to understand.

But crusts are easily destroyed. Grazing livestock and people who wander off of trails can break up fragile upper layers. That's why a "Don't Bust the Crust" program is underway to educate visitors to respect the desert's living surface.

GEOLOGICAL FORMATIONS

Devil's Tower

Mesas and buttes aren't the only unusual-looking formations created by wind, water, and chemical action. Other stone formations are made of hard volcanic rock that was left standing after all the softer rock around them was weathered away. A good example of this is Devil's Tower in Utah—the place where aliens landed in the movie *Close Encounters of the Third Kind*. And "pedestal rocks" are even stranger. They look like gigantic mushrooms. Scientists believe that salt and wind helped wear away their bases.

Desert Varnish

In some deserts, the boulders shine with a brown or black metallic coating that looks like it was painted on. But desert varnish is formed by colonies of microscopic bacteria that live on the rock surface. The bacteria absorb small amounts of iron, clay, and manganese from the atmosphere. Then they deposit it in layers that build up over thousands of years. The clay particles in the mixture shade the bacteria from the sun.

Fossils: Exposed conditions also make it easier for scientists and amateurs to find **fossils** in the desert. As the unprotected rock weathers away, the layers containing signs and remains of long-vanished life gradually come to the surface.

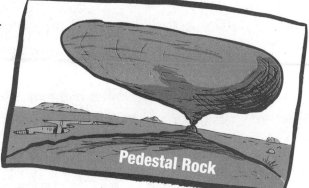
Pedestal Rock

Paleontologists have found remains of ancient whales in Egypt and penguins as big as a man in Peru. The first dinosaur eggs ever identified were uncovered in the Gobi desert of China. And in 2008, two new dinosaurs, a flying pterosaur and a plant-eating sauropod 65 feet (20 meters) long, were discovered in the Sahara.

Meteorites: In remote areas where the surface is sandy or smooth without a lot of pebbles or gravel, an unusual rock has a good chance of being a **meteorite** from outer space. They're often heavier than earth rocks, so they're less likely to blow away in desert winds. Their dark color also makes them stand out against light-colored sand, limestone, or salt surfaces. The best place to look for meteorites is in a **strewn field** like the Gold Basin in the Mojave Desert or the Nullarbor Plain in Australia.

But even in the desert, meteorites are rare. Most are tiny, though every now and then you can find a whopper.

WORDS TO KNOW

fossil: rocks with the remains or imprint of prehistoric life.

paleontologist: a scientist who studies fossils.

meteorite: a rocky or metallic object from space that lands on the earth.

strewn field: an area where meteorites have fallen.

—FASCINATING FACT—

One of archaeology's greatest mysteries is the Nazca Lines in Peru. Nobody knows why pictures of hummingbirds, spiders, monkeys, and llamas—as well as strange two-headed humanoids—were drawn on the Nazca Desert floor. All we know is that the lines were created between 500 BCE and 500 CE by local people. They were created by removing dark stones covering the desert to reveal the lighter bedrock underneath. The drawings are so large that you can only really see them from the air. By the time scientists realized that the Nazca Lines were ancient works of art, a highway had already been built right through one, a giant drawing of a lizard. But it's not true, as one writer claimed in the 1960s, that they were designed as landing strips for UFOs!

The second largest meteorite ever found in the U.S. was discovered in 1975 by some gold prospectors in the California desert. It was 3 feet (1 meter) around and weighed over 3 tons (2,700 kilograms). A Marine helicopter had to be used to retrieve the meteorite from its mountain location. It can now be seen at the California Desert Information Center in Barstow, California.

HISTORICAL AND ARCHAEOLOGICAL LANDMARKS

The desert traveler who wants to see ancient historical sites has lots to choose

from. Two of the most famous are the pyramids in Egypt and the ancient city of Timbuktu.

The pyramids have been a major tourist attraction since the time of the ancient Greeks. Built around 2,700 BCE, these massive structures were constructed out of huge stone blocks. Scientists still don't know exactly how the pyramids were built. Nor do they understand the meaning of the pyramid design.

The pyramids are essentially tombs. Inside are the mummified remains of the Pharaohs. Ancient Egyptians considered these rulers of Egypt to be descended from the gods. The largest pyramid is the Great Pyramid of Pharaoh Khufu. It stands 450 feet high and covers 13 acres.

Many people believe Timbuktu is a mythical place. But there is a real Timbuktu on the southern edge of the Sahara Desert in Mali that was founded about 1100 CE. Timbuktu was a major stop for traders passing through the desert for over 600 years. It was also a center of Muslim learning and home to one of the world's first universities. But when European merchant ships found a sailing route around Africa, traders stopped using the desert routes, and Timbuktu was virtually abandoned.

Today, shifting desert sands threaten to swallow many of the city's old schools, libraries and **mosques**. But the few remaining inhabitants of Timbuktu still guard many of the ancient books and documents, hidden inside their homes in chests and closets. These Arabic manuscripts are the city's greatest treasure. More and more historians are now beginning to rescue them from their hiding places and study them. And they're finding out things they never knew about African science, law, religion, government, and its long history of civilization.

WORDS TO KNOW

mosque: a building where Muslims gather to worship.

pilgrim: someone making a religious journey to a holy site.

hajj: a religious journey Muslims make to Mecca in present-day Saudi Arabia.

avalanche: sand, rock, snow, or other material moving quickly down a mountainside.

SACRED SITES

Pilgrims have traveled to the desert for ages. Outsiders sometimes have a hard time visiting religious desert sites—but there are always those who try. For Muslims, making the **hajj** to Mecca in Saudi Arabia is one of the required five pillars of faith. Every year millions of pilgrims travel to the birthplace of Islam's founder Mohammed for the five-day celebration. It includes a visit to the Kaaba.

Singing Sand and Booming Dunes

Singing sand dunes have puzzled desert travelers for centuries. Those who have heard the eerie sounds describe them as a boom, croak, bark, squeak, or low hum that can be heard for miles. When the Italian explorer Marco Polo passed through China's Taklamakan Desert in 1271, he wrote, "It often seems to you that you hear many instruments sounding, and especially drums. One night I heard, three times, a terrible noise, like crying, like someone dying."

In places like the Kelso Dunes in Mojave National Preserve in California, visitors like to run down the dunes to set them singing. Scientists used to think that creating a mini-**avalanche** made the dunes boom. But recently they discovered that all you need are the right kind of sand grains: smooth, round, and all the same size. Just shaking a jar of this kind of sand in the laboratory creates noisy vibrations. One scientist said it sounded "as though the jar were farting in your hand!"

SAY "EXCUSE ME."

Prrt!

= Shake = Shake

This is a cubical building containing an ancient black meteorite. Non-Muslims are forbidden in Mecca, but many have tried to sneak in. In 1853, the British adventurer Richard Francis Burton became famous for slipping into Mecca disguised as an Afghan Muslim.

— FASCINATING FACT —
French airplane pilot Antoine de Saint-Exupéry once made an emergency landing in the Sahara Desert. He found himself on an isolated plateau that was covered with meteorites the size of his hand. Saint-Exupéry went on to write the famous children's book *The Little Prince*, about a stranded pilot in the desert who comes upon a little boy who fell from another planet.

Other holy sites in the Middle East are shared by Islam, Christianity, and Judaism. Many believe that Mount Horeb in Egypt is the site of Mount Sinai. According to the Bible, that is where God spoke to the prophet Moses when he freed the Jewish people from slavery. Christians built a monastery there, which contains a shrub said to be descended from the Bible's burning bush. Moses is also an important prophet in the Islamic tradition. After Mohammed visited and gave the monastery his protection, a small mosque was created on the grounds. Today members of all three faiths come to see the site.

WORDS TO KNOW

shaman: a spiritual leader trained in a group's traditions and healing rituals.

Other cultures make desert pilgrimages too. In Mexico, the Huichol Indians walk into the Chihuahua Desert several times a year to gather peyote. They use the tiny cactus to produce religious visions. Along the way, **shamans** pass along knowledge of the land and traditions through chants, storytelling, and rituals. Tourists have come in and destroyed many peyote plants, which can take 10 to 30 years to grow back. So the government passed new rules to protect the Huichol's sacred cactus.

Uluru (also known as Ayers Rock) is a 1,000-foot-high (300-meter) mound of sandstone, one of the most famous landmarks in the Australian Outback. The Anangu, or Aborigines, are the original owners. The route to the top has special meaning to the Anangu. The view is magnificent, but the climb is dangerous. Some 35 visitors have died on the rock, a fact that saddens its Anangu caretakers.

Uluru (Ayers Rock)

Famous Desert Travelers

Crossing the desert shows that you're ready to face extreme temperatures, rough terrain, and sometimes-hostile inhabitants. But most of all, it makes for some great stories.

One of the earliest desert tourists to write about his adventures was Marco Polo. He was only 17 when he set out from Venice, Italy, to visit the Mongol leader Kublai Khan in 1271. With his father and uncle, Marco Polo traveled along the **Silk Road**. They passed through several deserts in Persia, Afghanistan, India, and China. In the Taklamakan Desert, the Polos hired camels to carry the food and supplies they would need for their treacherous crossing. "This desert is reported to be so long that it would take a year to go from end to end; and at the narrowest point it takes a month to cross it," Marco Polo later wrote. "It consists entirely of mountains and sands and valleys. There is nothing at all to eat." His tales of hardship and adventure helped spark Medieval Europe's age of exploration.

Abu Abdallah Ibn Battuta was a Muslim lawyer who left Morocco in northern Africa to make the hajj to Mecca in 1325. He ended up traveling around the Islamic world for the next 30 years. His book, called *A Gift to Those Who Contemplate the Wonders of Cities and the Marvels of Traveling*, describes a **caravan** journey across the Sahara to a town where the buildings were made of blocks of salt.

In 1861 the American writer Mark Twain took a horse-drawn stagecoach to the Nevada Territory. He didn't enjoy the trip. When the coach got stuck in a sandy desert, all the passengers had to get out and walk for 40 miles (65 kilometers)—with no water. "From one extremity of this desert to the other," Twain later wrote, "the road was white with the bones of oxen and horses."

For other travelers of that time, the desert had a romantic appeal. In 1883, before he became president, Theodore Roosevelt wrote about North Dakota for newspapers back East. "There are few sensations I prefer to that of galloping over these rolling limitless prairies," he said, "or winding my way among the barren, fantastic and grimly picturesque deserts of the so-called Bad Lands."

Women began exploring deserts on their own, too. In 1923 Rose Wilder Lane (the daughter of the author of *Little House on the Prairie*) crossed the Syrian desert by motor car. Her group got lost and she and the other women had to help stand guard against nighttime bandits. Gertrude Bell rode camels and ate sheep's eyes with Arab tribespeople as she studied historical ruins. After World War I, she was part of a British group who helped create the present-day country of Iraq.

29

WORDS TO KNOW

Silk Road: an ancient trade route across Asia between China and the Mediterranean.

caravan: travelers leading a train of pack animals through the desert.

CHAPTER 3

Getting Around in the Desert

It takes special adaptations for people, animals, and machines to cross the desert by land. Desert travelers can choose from many different ways of getting around. Here's a look at some of the options.

UNDER YOUR OWN STEAM

Walking: The simplest way to explore the desert is by foot. But in this hot, dry, barren environment, there's no such thing as a casual stroll. So consider every walk into the desert a hike, and prepare accordingly.

Specialized desert clothing, sturdy boots, and a backpack to carry your supplies are a must. These will be discussed in later chapters. But before you head out, you'll need to get in shape for the strenuous journey ahead. There are also some walking tricks you can learn that will help you travel across the desert's rough terrain.

IT'S JUST LIKE WALKING UP STAIRS!

KICK!

—FASCINATING FACT—

On sand dunes, try to walk on the **windward** side. The side facing the wind is firmer and more tightly packed than the **leeward** side, which is looser and more slippery.

30

No matter what kind of desert you're visiting, the landscape can make traveling slow going. On hills, loose rocks and gravel make it easy to slip and stumble. Steep, narrow canyons can meander around like a maze, taking you back and forth across many miles before you reach your destination. They are also dangerous to hike in because of the chance of flash floods.

Walking on flat land can be difficult too. Hard rocky surfaces can tire out your feet. You'll also need to watch out for stones in your path. In some places such as lava beds, the rocks may be so big that you'll find yourself stepping carefully from boulder to boulder.

When you're hiking—and especially when you're in a hot desert—you should use walking techniques that are as efficient as possible. The less work your body has to do to take a step, the more steps you'll be able to take. You'll also sweat less, which means you won't use up your water as quickly. (There's more about how much you should drink in the desert later in the book.)

One trick to try is to walk in a line, so the person in front breaks a trail for the rest of the group. Trade off being first. Instead of walking up and down over sand dunes or rocky hills, pick a route that stays on top of the highest part of the ridge. You'll save energy, even if it means going a little farther. And when you do go up or down, try to **traverse** or zigzag the steepest part of the hill instead of tackling it head-on.

WORDS TO KNOW

windward: side facing the wind.

leeward: side facing away from the wind.

traverse: a zigzag way up or down a steep hill.

Traverse

31

SUN PROTECTION

AS MUCH
H₂O AS POSSIBLE

SPECIAL
SEALED TIRES

Bicycling: If walking isn't fast enough for you, consider bringing your bicycle to the desert. Road bikes and mountain bikes are both popular ways of exploring desert land. But as with other means of transportation, desert biking requires extra precautions and a few special adaptations. Carry as many water bottles as will fit on your bike's frame—at least a gallon a day. A bike repair kit is a must as well. And guard against thorny plants by using a tire sealant in your inner tubes.

TRY THIS: make sand gaiters

Runners in the Gobi Desert Challenge use **gaiters** to keep sand out of their shoes. Modern gaiters are made of lightweight rip-stop nylon and have elastic at the top. The Gobi Challenge models come in gold and blaze orange. If you don't have gaiters, you can make an old-fashioned substitute called **puttees** to protect your shoes and legs.

SUPPLIES

- 2 elastic bandages or strips of old cloth about 3 inches (7 centimeters) wide and about 6 feet (2 meters) long

WORDS TO KNOW

gaiters: cloth shoe coverings that reach up to the knee.

puttees: cloth strips wrapped around the leg from ankle to knee.

1 Roll up the strip of bandage or cloth. Begin wrapping at the front of your shoe. Overlap the top of your shoe with the bandage. Go around a few times until the opening of the shoe is completely covered.

2 Continue wrapping the bandage up your leg. If you want to make a criss-cross pattern, angle the bandage as you wrap. Don't make it too tight! If you're wearing long pants, wrap it right over the pants.

3 Keep going until you reach your knee or run out of fabric. Tuck the top of the bandage under so it stays tight. Wrap your other leg the same way.

Teenager Finishes Footrace in the Gobi

In 2007, a 16-year-old runner from Scotland named Jonathan Graham finished eighth in the Sandbaggers Gobi Challenge, a 140-mile race in southern Mongolia. Jonathan was one of 23 racers who set out across broiling deserts and Asia's highest sand dunes in temperatures of more than 104 degrees Fahrenheit (40 degrees Celsius). His feat put him in the record books as the youngest person to ever run across the Gobi Desert.

The race was grueling. Competitors had to carry emergency supplies with them, including food, a sleeping bag, compass, and first aid kit. They were given water along the way, and slept at night in the tents of local goat herders.

"The land was so harsh, there was no water and we were completely on our own," Jonathan told a reporter. "The wind would blow sand into the tent and I never got more than a couple of hours sleep."

On day three Jonathan ran into problems when he drank too much water. "I was staggering around and wasn't sure where I was," he said.

Then, on day five, he went off the route and got lost. Luckily he found his way back again, but medical technicians had to treat him for blisters. But by the last day Jonathan was in such good shape that he was the first person to cross the finish line, making him the winner of the final stage of the race. As each of the other racers came in, he even played the bagpipes for them! His accomplishment was covered in Scottish newspapers and raised money for Marie Curie Cancer Care in memory of a friend who had died of a brain tumor.

ANIMAL POWER

Animals were the first means of transportation in the desert, and they're still used by many people living in remote parts of the world, where gasoline and repair shops are hard to come by. But they're also popular with travelers who want to see the desert the traditional way. Animals do less harm to the fragile desert environment than big-wheeled all-terrain vehicles, too.

Camels: Camels are the perfect animals for trips over the desert. They can walk 30 miles (50 kilometers) a day and carry 300 pounds (136 kilograms) or more. With saddles, camels can be ridden like horses. But unlike horses, camels will kneel down so you can get on!

Camels have been used as pack animals for thousands of years. Caravans with lines of camels 6 miles (10 kilometers) long once carried spices, incense, and other goods throughout the Middle East and Central Asia. And they're still used today for transport in a few desert areas. In Mali, caravans 3,000 camels strong carry salt hundreds of miles from mines to Timbuktu.

— FASCINATING FACT —

Scientists believe that ancestors of the camel came from North America. They migrated northwest into Asia and south to the Andes Mountains. So the llama of South America, which is also frequently used as a desert pack animal, is a distant cousin of the camel.

Practice Walking Over Sand Dunes

Here's a special technique for walking on loose, slanted surfaces. As you go to take a step, instead of putting your foot flat against the slope of the sand dune, dig out a little ledge to stand on by kicking your toe straight ahead. This is called a kick step.

Kick Step

Next, put your weight on this leg, straighten your knee until you're standing, and pause a moment. This is called a rest step. Then do the same thing with your other foot, continuing on at an even pace until you reach the top of the sand dune.

To come down, you'll use a plunge step. With your foot parallel to the ground, kick straight down into the sand with your heel, making a little ledge to stand on. Take a rest, and then do the same with the other foot until you reach the bottom.

Plunge Step

This technique also works when walking on hilly land covered in gravel or loose stones. You can even practice it in the snow! Mountain climbers use the kick step, rest step, and plunge step as they walk up snow-capped peaks.

Horses: Another good choice for desert travel is the horse. The Bedouin people particularly prized their Arabian breed of horses for use in battle. When European explorers introduced horses to North America, they were quickly adopted by the Native Americans of the desert.

The Mongolian horse has been used in the Gobi Desert since the days of Genghis Khan. Although smaller than other horses, Mongolian horses can walk 30 miles (50 kilometers) a day, and a cart pulled by four of them can haul as much as 2 tons (1.8 metric tons) of cargo.

Unlike camels, however, horses need water every day—more than 10 gallons (38 liters) of it. So don't take your horse across the desert unless you know where the water sources are!

Primitive Horses Making a Comeback in the Gobi

Named after a Russian general, Przewalski's Horse is a primitive species of horse that once roamed the Gobi desert. But harsh conditions and competition for grazing land from sheep, goats, and other livestock nearly drove them into extinction in the 1900s. Happily, zoos and wildlife centers have been breeding these horses from a handful of survivors in captivity. Today, as their numbers increase, Przewalski's Horses are being reintroduced into the wild.

These wild horses are very different looking from modern horses. They are short and squat, with big heads, and shaggy brown coats. Their black manes stand up stiffly like those of donkeys or zebras.

In areas where Przewalski's Horses are being released, the local people are careful not to let their modern horses breed with the wild horses. This is so the wild horses can continue to live as a separate species. But because many of the same conditions that almost wiped them out before still exist, Przewalski's Horses will continue to need help and protection for some time to come.

Mules: A cross between a horse and a donkey, mules have qualities that make them good desert animals. They are three times as strong as a horse, more sure-footed, intelligent, and trainable. While "stubborn as a mule" is an accurate way to describe their personalities, mule lovers say this is their way of protecting themselves. Mule rides into the Grand Canyon are popular.

Burros: Public lands in the American Southwest are filled with wild burros. Spanish explorers brought wild asses from Africa as work animals in the 1500s. Despite their small size, burros can carry up to 200 pounds (90 kilograms)! During the 1800s, pack burros carried tools for gold prospectors and hauled ore out of mines.

— FASCINATING FACT —

Students at Edith Teter Elementary School in Colorado are behind a movement to make pack burro racing the official state sport. Inspired by old-time prospectors, the game calls for burros to carry a pick, shovel, and gold pan. Riding the burro is strictly forbidden, but racers can push, pull, or carry their animal to the finish line, if necessary.

When the Gold Rush was over, many burros returned to the wild. Although tourists love them, today wild burros are considered a nuisance. They trample creek beds and consume food and water needed by native wildlife. So every year the U.S. Bureau of Land Management gathers up thousands of wild burros and horses to be adopted by individuals and humane groups.

MOTORIZED DESERT TRAVEL

Most desert driving, especially in the United States, is done on paved roads. But even on a highway, a desert traveler needs to be prepared. Cars need to be in good working order. Taking along some basic tools for jumping a dead battery or fixing a flat is important. Having at least 5 gallons (20 liters) of water per person—and extra water in case the car's radiator overheats—could save your life. Some drivers like to bring a gas can with extra fuel as well.

Setting Land Speed Records

The fastest place on Earth may be the Bonneville Salt Flats. This is a dry lakebed 12 miles (19 kilometers) long in the Great Salt Lake basin in Utah. The salt flats attract racecar drivers from around the world looking to set land speed records. This is possible because the surface is a hard, smooth, white crust made of halite (common table salt) and other minerals left every spring after the winter's flood waters evaporate.

The first unofficial record to be set at the Bonneville Salt Flats was in 1914, when Teddy Tetzlaff drove a Blitzen Benz piston engine motorcar 142 miles (230 kilometers) per hour. In 1965 Craig Breedlove went 601 miles (967 kilometers) per hour in the jet-powered *Spirit of America*. And in 1970 Gary Gabolich guided a rocket car called the *Blue Flame* to a record-setting 622 miles (1,001 kilometers) per hour.

FASCINATING FACT

In 1982, the son of Margaret Thatcher, who was the British Prime Minister, caused an international stir. His tiny sports car broke down in the Sahara desert during the Paris-Dakar rally, a race from France to western Africa. Mark Thatcher and his two teammates were stranded for six days with minimal supplies before Algerian search teams rescued them.

Driving off-road or on dirt roads in the desert requires a special vehicle. It must have high clearance to get over rocks and other small obstacles. The tires must be wide and rugged to spread out the weight and stay on top of the sand. And the vehicle should have four-wheel drive for getting out of ruts and dealing with slippery conditions.

WORDS TO KNOW

corrode: to eat away at metal gradually by chemical action.

Driving on sand in a regular car is not a good idea. But if you're forced to, let some air out of the tires to increase their surface area. Also, avoid quick stops and starts and sharp turns. This will keep the wheels from digging into the sand and getting stuck.

Dry riverbeds and salt lakes can be hazardous too. Stick to the middle of the salt flats, where the crust is thickest. Watch out for puddles of salt water, which can short out your car's electrical system. Also avoid pressure ridges that can scrape the bottom of your car. Be sure to wash off any salt that sticks to your car as soon as possible. The salt can **corrode** the metal body.

Off-road driving has become a favorite tourist activity in deserts around the world. Dune buggies are lightweight, fat-tired vehicles designed to drive over sand. They're not only popular on drive-yourself group tours, they are also used by the U.S. Border Patrol.

In Dubai on the Arabian Peninsula, you can rent a dune buggy at age 15. In Arizona, kids can book a birthday party drive into the Sonoran Desert. But even on these fun rides, care must be taken. In 2008 Australia closed a park in the Simpson Desert for the summer because of the number of accidents and deaths involving foreign visitors out for a drive. Vehicles can also disturb wild-life and permanently mark up the landscape. They can even cause worldwide environmental damage. One expert says the "Toyota-ization" of the desert in recent years has resulted in 10 times more dust entering the atmosphere from Africa as was found half a century ago.

FASCINATING FACT

Dune buggies were originally made from stripped-down Volkswagen Beetles.

Tanks in the Desert

Armored tanks, like those used in wars in the Middle East, are much bigger and heavier than four-wheel-drive vehicles. But tanks actually cause less destruction to the desert surface. That's because tanks move along on long rubber treads instead of wheels. The treads help distribute the tank's weight over a larger surface, which puts less pressure on the ground.

Even tanks can do serious damage, though. During World War II, U.S. General George S. Patton used the Mojave Desert to train tank crews for fighting in North Africa. More than 50 years later, the tracks are still visible. A study by the U.S. Army suggested it could take 200 to 1,000 years for the damaged area to recover completely.

TRY THIS: Design a desert transport

Now that you know a little about getting around in the desert, can you come up with your own design for a desert transport?

SUPPLIES

- pencil and paper
- building toys
- recycled materials such as cardboard boxes, bottle tops, rubber tubes, colored cellophane, etc.
- scissors, tape, brad fasteners for attaching wheels, etc.

1 Think about what a desert vehicle should have. Would it roll on wheels, would it hover, or would it crawl? Would it have a sun roof—or a sunshade? Is it powered with rockets, sails, or solar panels? How about adding tinted windows, air conditioning, and a built-in refrigerator for cold drinks?

2 Describe your desert vehicle in words or pictures. Now, build a model of your new vehicle using materials from around the house.

Route 66

Route 66 was once the most famous highway in America. It was the subject of a song, a hit TV show, and numerous movies (including the animated film Cars). Built in the 1920s, the road passed through the Southwestern desert on its way from Chicago, Illinois, to Los Angeles, California.

By the 1950s, Route 66 beckoned tourists with teepee-shaped motels, frozen custard stands, reptile farms, and drive-in movie theaters. But within 30 years it had largely been replaced by more modern roads. Today, local and international groups are working to preserve the route and restore the communities it once supported.

Sandboarding

If you like snowboarding, you'll love sandboarding. Sand parks can be found in deserts around the world, including Dubai, Australia, Namibia, Japan, Chile, and the western United States. Of course, with all that gritty sand flying around, you'll want to wear eye protection, and maybe use a board with a stainless steel bottom. And instead of a snow suit you'll wear sand socks and board shorts!

TRAVEL BY WATER

A trip down the Colorado River is one of the most breathtaking ways to see the Grand Canyon. From Lee's Ferry to Lake Mead is over 250 miles (402 kilometers), and many of the rapids along the way are legendary. Almost 30,000 people go every year on voyages lasting from one to 25 days. You can float in a raft, paddle a kayak, or motor down in a craft called a J-Rig. But you need a permit to travel through the Grand Canyon, so sign up with a commercial tour company or put your name on the waiting list for a private trip. It can take years on the waiting list, so plan ahead.

TRAVEL BY WIND POWER

Playas and other flat, empty desert terrain are perfect for landsailers and kite buggies. Landsailers are three-wheeled vehicles that look like surfboards or go-carts with a sail attached. Kite buggies are similar, except they're pulled by a huge kite that's tied to the vehicle. On hard dry surfaces these vehicles can hit 40–65 miles (65–105 kilometers) per hour.

CHAPTER 4

Water, the Most Important Resource

Without water you won't get very far in the desert. In 100-degree-Fahrenheit heat (38 degrees Celsius), just walking can cause you to lose a quart (just under a liter) of perspiration an hour. By the time you start to feel very thirsty, **dehydration** can already be setting in. The next sign is crankiness, weakness, and nausea. Soon your head will ache and you'll feel dizzy, confused, and disoriented. Your tongue will swell and your vision will be affected. After three to five days with no water, you can die.

WORDS TO KNOW

dehydration: the unhealthy loss of fluid in the body.

So having enough water in the desert is literally a matter of life and death. The best solution is to carry all the water you need. Some experts recommend a gallon (4 liters) per day. Others advise taking twice as much. In his book *Desert Survivor*, wilderness guide John Annerino says he drank up to 5 gallons (20 liters) a day when he hiked across the Baja California desert in Mexico in 106-degree-Fahrenheit heat (41 degrees Celsius).

Of course, on longer trips—or in an emergency survival situation—you'll need to find water yourself. Some desert water sources will be obvious. For others, you'll have to learn some of the tricks that native desert people, plants, and animals use to find water that's hidden from view.

FASCINATING FACT

The ancient Nabataeans collected rainwater using an advanced system of water channels, pipes, and underground holding tanks. Like the buildings in their cities, these were carved right into the rocky cliffs.

Rules for Using and Saving Water in the Desert

- There's an old desert saying: the best container for water is your body. So when your water is running low, don't ration it. Drink up!
- Drink before you're thirsty. Remind yourself to take sips at regular intervals, whether you feel like it or not.
- Take it easy when the sun is hottest. You'll save water by traveling in the morning and evening, and finding shade or covering up in the middle of the day,
- Don't eat when you're thirsty. Your body uses water to digest food.

DESERT RIVERS

In general, water is scarce in the desert. But at certain times and in certain places you'll find plenty. Empty streambeds fill up during heavy rains, creating **ephemeral** rivers. But it's **perennial** rivers like the Colorado that are the most reliable source of water in the desert. Other examples include the Tigris and Euphrates Rivers in Iraq, and the Indus River in India. Perennial rivers start in the moist highland regions and flow down into arid lowlands. As they wind their way through the desert, they create long, narrow strips of green in a land of rock and sand.

WORDS TO KNOW

ephemeral: lasting a very short time.
perennial: present throughout the whole year.

pothole: small, temporary desert pool.
estivate: when the body slows down during hot weather.

Temporary Pools: A sudden heavy downpour can also create a desert **pothole**. This is a dip in the rocky floor that fills up with rain. While that sounds handy for a thirsty hiker, a pothole is basically just an oversized puddle. It can quickly become murky with dead leaves, animal droppings, algae, and other organic stuff.

What's nasty for you, however, is great for other desert creatures. A wide variety of desert animals spend their whole lives in these temporary pools. For example, the spadefoot toad can go from egg to tadpole to toadlet in just nine days!

Once the pond dries up, some animals **estivate**, or sleep, until the next rainfall. Some spadefoot toads burrow into the mud, and develop a covering of old dead skin. This holds in moisture. When the rain returns, the toad digs its way out of the ground and sheds its dried-out skin.

Lungfish from Africa and South America can estivate for as long as three years. When its pool evaporates, the lungfish can breathe using its swim bladder, an organ that fish can fill with air. Most fish just use their swim bladder to help them float at a particular depth underwater, but the lungfish can use it to take in oxygen from the air. To keep itself moist, the lungfish burrows into the mud. Then it covers itself in a mucus sac and breathes through a mucus tube.

FASCINATING FACT

The organisms in a pothole are very sensitive to sudden change. If you disturb the water by swimming in it, or drinking it, you can change the chemistry or temperature enough to harm the inhabitants. Avoid using pothole water. And try not to step in a dry pothole.

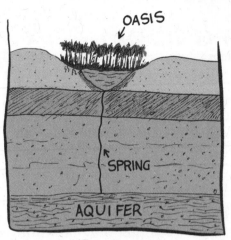

OASES

An **oasis** is so rare and wonderful that its name is used for any place that lets you escape stressful surroundings. Most oases (the plural for oasis) develop around **springs** or lakes fed by water from underground.

In some places, this underground water comes from rain that falls on nearby hills and mountains. This water soaks into the ground and slowly seeps downhill along an **aquifer**, which is an absorbent layer of rock, sand, or gravel.

In other places, the water comes from an **artesian aquifer**. This is an absorbent layer of rock that's sandwiched between two waterproof layers. As water flows downhill, it gets trapped here. Eventually, so much pressure builds up that the water is forced to the surface wherever there are openings. Sometimes the water will pool and form a lake. People also dig artesian wells for a reliable source of water that rises to the surface on its own.

> **─FASCINATING FACT─**
> Remember the rule of three—you can survive three weeks without food, but only three days without water.

Water flows very slowly in artesian aquifers. It can also be quite old. For example, the water in the Great Artesian Basin in Australia's interior desert is almost 2 million years old.

WORDS TO KNOW

oasis: a green, fertile area surrounded by desert.

spring: a source of water that comes from underground.

aquifer: an absorbent layer of rock, sand, or gravel that carries water underground.

artesian aquifer: an aquifer squeezed between two waterproof layers, putting the water under high pressure.

—FASCINATING FACT—

The water that spurts out of the Great Artesian Basin in Australia is hot—between 90 degrees Fahrenheit (32 degrees Celsius) and boiling. That's convenient if you'd like some tea, but not if you want a drink from the tap! The water isn't heated by the blazing desert sun, however. It's heated by **geothermal** energy when it comes into contact with hot rock deep within the earth's core. Scientists are studying ways to use that energy to provide power for other parts of Australia.

Many oases are nothing more than a little pond with a few palm trees around. But many are large enough to supply water to an entire city and its surrounding farmland. The city of Bukhara, Uzbekistan, in Central Asia, for example, started as an ancient oasis trading post. Today it has over a million residents.

WORDS TO KNOW

geothermal: heated by the earth's inner core.

qanat: an underground water canal.

irrigation: bringing water to a dry area to help grow crops.

QANATS

A **qanat** is an ancient **irrigation** system that is still used today in many parts of the Middle East and Asia. It was invented nearly 3,000 years ago by the Persians in present-day Iran.

A qanat is an underground canal that brings water from the highlands down into the lower desert. Qanats have stairways so residents can climb down to reach the underground chambers. These rooms are sometimes used for bathing. On the surface, openings are made so that water can be drawn up for drinking. Eventually the canal emerges above ground, where the water is used for irrigating the fields.

In their heyday, qanats spread to the Roman Empire, Spain, China, and South America. Slaves were often used for the difficult and dangerous work of building and maintaining a qanat. They had to repair the damage done by flash floods, and clean out the sand and debris that fell into the ventilation shafts. But as slavery disappeared, many qanat systems were abandoned.

Qanats are still used today in certain areas. Some are owned by all the residents in a town and shared equally. Volunteers often tend the qanat today for the good of the community. Other qanats are privately owned and the water is **leased** to those who want it. There are water lease contracts still in force that were written 800 years ago!

The United Nations is working to bring back this traditional water management system to areas that could benefit from its simple but ingenious technology.

FRESHWATER LAKES

As the Ice Age ended thousands of years ago, the climate grew wetter and many freshwater desert lakes were formed. For example, a vast prehistoric body of water called Lake Bonneville covered much of present-day Utah, Nevada, and Idaho. But today all that's left is the Great Salt Lake in Utah.

Most freshwater desert lakes now in existence were artificially created by dams, which back up rivers. One of the most famous dams is the Hoover Dam, constructed in the 1930s on the Colorado River. It created Lake Mead, a **reservoir** that supplies water to southern California.

WORDS TO KNOW

leased: a contract giving someone rights to use another person's property for a specific amount of time in return for a payment.

reservoir: an artificial lake used for collecting water.

make a mirage

In this demonstration you can see light rays bend as they go from lower-density air to higher-density water. The object you're looking at will appear to be floating upside down above the table!

1 Make sure the water bottle is filled to the top, with no air inside. Put the top on tightly. Stack the books on the table.

2 Place the small object about 6 inches (15 centimeters) behind the stack of books. You should not be able to see it when the top of the book stack is at eye level.

3 Lay the bottle on its side behind the books, in front of the small object.

4 Look at the top of the stack again at eye level. Now you should be able to see the object, upside down. (If you can't see it, move it closer or farther away.)

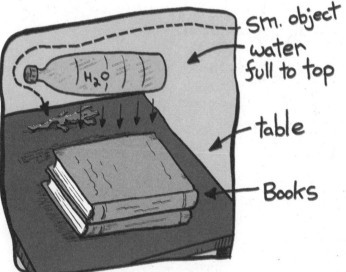

Sm. object

water full to top

table

Books

WORDS TO KNOW

mirage: an optical effect that looks like a pool of water, caused by bending light rays.

Problems can arise when a dam reduces the amount of water flowing into the desert. People living downstream from a dam often don't have enough water for drinking and farming. For example, when the Aswan Dam was built on the Nile River in Egypt, it eliminated the river's yearly floods. Those floods once fertilized farmlands naturally by depositing minerals onshore. Today, only a small fraction of the water that once passed through that part of the Nile Valley still flows. Without the floods, farmers have to buy fertilizer for their fields. And salt that was once washed away to the sea has built up in the river to the point where the water can't be used for drinking or farming.

WORDS TO KNOW

horizon: where the earth and the sky meet in a landscape.

density: the amount of a material there is in a particular amount of space.

FASCINATING FACT

Much of the world's table salt is harvested from salt lakes and seas.

Mirage

Sometimes people trudging through the desert glimpse a pool of clear, shimmering water on the **horizon**. But as they approach the spot, there's nothing there but heat waves coming off the desert floor. It's not a practical joke—it's a mirage.

A mirage isn't a figment of your imagination, but a trick of the light. In the desert, air near the ground is often hotter than it is at eye level. And air of different temperatures also has different **density**. As light waves travel from the air of one density to another, it bends.

So your brain sees two images—the real one from the light waves coming straight at you, and an upside-down version bending back up at you from the ground. Voila! You're got yourself a mirage.

48

TRY THIS: Use a Solar Still to Desalinate Water

This solar still catches condensation from a container of salty water and directs it into a separate container. As the still warms up, water vapor rises, hits the plastic wrap, and condenses back into drops of water. The drops slide down the plastic wrap into the clean container. These drops are pure water. The salt—which is too heavy to evaporate—is left behind.

SUPPLIES

- two containers, one smaller and shorter than the other
- water
- salt
- stand to hold the smaller container, like a canning jar ring or cookie cutter
- clear plastic wrap
- pebble, marble or other small weight
- rubber band or tape
- a sunny spot or desk lamp to heat the water

1 Make sure both containers are clean enough to drink from, inside and out.

2 Pour about 2 inches (5 centimeters) of water into the large container. Mix in a few spoonfuls of salt and stir until dissolved. Dip a finger in the water to taste how salty it is.

3 Put the stand in the salty water, and set the smaller container on it. The smaller container should still be lower than the edge of the larger container. Cover the whole thing with plastic wrap.

4 Place the small weight in the middle of the plastic wrap so that it dips down. It should almost touch the edge of the small cup. Smooth out as many wrinkles as you can and fasten the wrap with a rubber band or tape.

5 Put the solar still in the sun or under the lamp to warm. When you've collected some water in the smaller container, dip a finger in to taste if it's salty. Compare it to the water in the bottom of the large container. What changes do you notice?

Solar Still

Small Stone

Fresh water

Salt Water

49

— **FASCINATING FACT**—

About 30 different species of pupfish live in ponds around the American Southwest. All of them are descended from much larger fish that lived in Lake Bonneville during the last Ice Age. One species, the Devil's Hole pupfish, is found only in a very small, very deep pool in Death Valley National Park. It was one of the first animals to be named an Endangered Species. In 2006, only 38 were still alive, but its numbers are rising again thanks to protection from the U.S. Fish and Wildlife Service.

SALT LAKES

Most lakes in the desert are too salty for drinking or farming. When water flows in but doesn't flow out, it evaporates, and the salt minerals dissolved in the water become very **concentrated**, giving it a high **salinity**. Don Juan Pond in Antarctica is believed to be about 40 percent salt—so salty it doesn't freeze even at 58 degrees Fahrenheit below zero (-50 degrees Celsius).

WORDS TO KNOW

concentrated: a lot of one substance in a mixture.

salinity: the amount of salt in a mixture.

desalination: removing the salt.

In order for the water to be used for drinking or farming, it has to go through a process of **desalination**. There are desalination plants throughout the Middle East to provide drinking water for desert populations. And for the desert traveler, there are ways to desalinate small amounts of water for emergency use.

SALTY DENSE WATER!

The Dead Sea

The Great Salt Lake in Utah is too smelly for swimmers. The so-called "lake stink" comes from decaying algae on the shore. But tourists can take a dip in the Dead Sea between Israel and Jordan—although they tend to float, not swim. That's because there's so much salt dissolved in the water in the Dead Sea that it actually makes it thick enough to hold a person up. In fact, the density of the water is so high that many people bring a book to read while they float along . . .
no raft needed!

FOG AND DEW

FOG

Cool coastal deserts don't get much rain, but they do get fog. So the plants and animals there have adapted to make use of the mist and condensation. For example, the darkling beetle of the Namib Desert in Africa has microscopic ridges on its back. When fog blows in, beetles line up along the top of the sand dunes with their rear ends in the air. The fog is caught by the ridges and runs down their backs into their mouths. On a good night they can collect up to 40 percent of their weight in water.

The welwitschia plant, also found in the Namib Desert, has been called the ugliest plant in the world. Still, it's managed to survive thousands of years by absorbing mist and fog through two long leaves. The leaves grow out of a stem on the desert floor and just keep getting longer and longer, splitting into a dried, tangled pile on the sand. The water it gathers is stored in a gigantic taproot below the surface.

THAT'S ONE UGLY PLANT!

←TAPROOT

TRY THIS: SOAK UP THE MORNING DEW

See how much water you can capture with this survival technique. You'll need a cotton bandana or other piece of absorbent cloth, as well as a measuring cup. On a night when you're expecting the weather to be cool in the morning, lay the cloth outside where it won't be disturbed. The next day, check to see if it's wet. If it is, wring it out into the measuring cup. How much water did you obtain? How many bandanas full of dew would you need to last a day in the desert?

Plants and animals like these have inspired scientists to come up with methods of harvesting mist and fog for people to use. In the Atacama Desert town of Chungungo, Chile, for example, scientists set up a system of fog-catcher nets on the hillsides. The nets captured fog on their strands. The drops of water then ran down the strands into gutters leading down to the town. The system supplied all the water the town needed for many years before falling into disrepair. Now scientists are working on a system the townspeople can maintain themselves.

FINDING HIDDEN WATER

Maps may not be useful for finding water in the desert. Many lakes and streams are only full after a heavy rain. But if you pay close attention to the land and the inhabitants, there are ways to tell where water may be hiding.

- Look, or head, downhill. Any water pools left after the last rain will be in the dips and holes of desert valleys.
- Try digging for water at the bend of a dry riverbed. Just be alert for flash floods and have a quick way out.
- In marshy areas, dig a hole to see if it fills with water.
- Bees, ants, and mosquitoes indicate that water is nearby.
- Watch for plants and trees. They may be tapping into a spring or other underground water source.
- Birds and mammals usually head to water in the morning and evening. If a bird looks heavy and flaps its wings loudly, it may be full and heading back from the watering hole.
- Animal tracks and human trails will always lead to water, eventually.

Water Purification

Always purify water from natural sources by boiling it, adding iodine, or using a hiker's water filter. That will reduce your chances of getting sick from any waterborne germs. Some liquids—such as blood, urine, and radiator fluid from a car engine—cannot be made drinkable, even in an emergency. They have chemicals and minerals in them that are worse for your body than drinking nothing at all.

TRY THIS: use Bags to Capture Plant moisture

In an emergency, you can always trap water from green leaves using a plastic bag. As the leaves dry, the moisture they release will condense on the inside of the bag. You can also use a live plant. It will release water vapor in **transpiration**. Ask an adult to make sure the plant you use is safe for drinking.

SUPPLIES

- lettuce or other green leaves, or live houseplant, bush, or tree
- a clean, clear plastic bag
- twist-tie or string
- sunny spot or desk lamp

WORDS TO KNOW

transpiration: when a plant loses water vapor through the openings in its leaves and stem.

1 If you are using lettuce or other leaves or a small houseplant, put them in a plastic bag and close with the twist tie. If you are using a larger plant or a branch, cover the leaves with the plastic bag and close using twist-tie or string.

2 Place the bag in a sunny spot or under the heat of a desk lamp for several hours.

3 Check on your bag from time to time to see if water has started to collect on the inside of the bag.

4 If an adult says it is safe, taste the water inside the bag. With cut leaves, you can keep checking back to see if enough water collects to drink in a cup or sip through a straw.

5 Caution: Don't leave a live plant in the bag too long or you can kill it!

— FASCINATING FACT —

Cacti are full of water, but they don't make good sources of drinking water. Except for the fishhook barrel cactus, most cactus flesh is poisonous. But the fruit of saguaro and prickly pears cactus are juicy and safe. Other desert plants also hide moisture in their bark, roots, or fruit that can be used in a pinch by people and animals. They include date palms in the Middle East, baobab trees in Africa, saxaul in Central Asia, and bloodwood desert oaks and water trees in Australia.

CHAPTER 5

Clothing, Shelter, and Food

The best way to find out how to eat, sleep, and dress in the desert is to observe the people who live there. In many places, high-tech gear has taken over from the **traditional** way of doing things. But both modern and traditional approaches are based on the same principle: using the best materials at hand to make being in the desert as safe and comfortable as possible.

FASCINATING FACT

Archaeologists have found mummies wearing woolen shawls in Chile's Atacama Desert. They were left there by the ancient Chinchorro people. The Chinchorro began creating mummies of men, women, and children as early as 5000 BCE.

54

DRESSING FOR HEAT, COLD, AND SUN

Dressing in the desert is more than a matter of good looks. Desert clothing has to protect you, both from extremes in temperature and from the damaging rays of the sun.

Arab Muslims often cover themselves head-to-toe, both for protection from the elements and for modesty.

Men traditionally wear a long, loose-fitting white wool tunic that allows air to circulate. A headcloth called a **kaffiyeh** is held on by heavy rope-like coils. It can be wrapped around the face and neck to block the sun or sand. Women usually wear black robes. They cover their hair and sometimes their entire face with a scarf or veil. Leather sandals are the usual footwear on the hot sands.

WORDS TO KNOW

traditional: old way of doing things.

archaeologist: a scientist who studies ancient people and their cultures.

kaffiyeh: an Arab cloth head covering.

del: a long, loose jacket worn in Mongolia.

ethnic: a group whose members share a similar culture.

In Mongolia both men and women wear a garment called a **del**. It's a long jacket with a high collar and a sash around the waist. Every **ethnic** group has its own style. A cold weather del has a sheepskin lining and sleeves that hang down past the hands. Mongolians also wear several styles of hats, each with its own symbolic meaning, and boots with upturned toes. This is a Tibetan Buddhist custom to avoid hurting the earth.

― **FASCINATING FACT** ―

The Tuareg people, or "blue men" of North Africa, are famous for the deep **indigo** color of their clothing—and their fierceness. Once they made their living by attacking caravans traveling across the Sahara, covering their faces with heavy blue veils. In more recent times, before trucks made camels obsolete, they switched to leading caravans through the desert instead. Although today the Tuareg no longer need to hide their faces like masked bandits, some can still be seen wearing their blue veils and robes.

In hot deserts some cultures wear little or no clothing at all. The people often have dark skin that gives them some protection from the sun, like the Khoisan people of the Kalahari Desert in southern Africa and the Aboriginal people of Australia.

Some ancient Native Americans wore only an apron (for women) or a **breechcloth** (for men), which they wove from plants or hair. In winter they added blankets, shirts, and robes. Native Americans also wore sandals that were braided or woven from yucca fibers. Juniper bark was used for socks—and for diapers.

WORDS TO KNOW

indigo: a deep purplish-blue color.

breechcloth: a cloth worn about the waist as clothing in warm climates.

Does Color Make You Cooler?

Something black in the sun usually gets hotter than something white. This is because black absorbs light and white reflects it. So is white clothing cooler than black clothing? Perhaps, but many Arab people wear black robes. It turns out the color of the clothing doesn't make much difference, as long as the garment is loose enough to allow a breeze between clothes and skin.

TRY THIS: make a Foreign Legion Hat

The French Foreign Legion was an extra-tough fighting unit formed in 1831 in the deserts of North Africa. Legionaries wore a distinctive hat, called a **kepi**. It had a flat top and a flap down the back to keep the neck and ears cool and shaded from the sun. The Foreign Legion–style hat is still popular today.

SUPPLIES

- newspaper or scrap paper to protect your work surface
- painter's cap (available at paint stores or craft supply stores) or old baseball cap
- measuring tape or ruler
- pencil
- scissors
- lightweight fabric
- iron
- glue (use fabric glue if you want the hat to be washable)

1 Cover your workspace with newspaper or scrap paper. Put on the hat so the bottom edge is straight, not tilted. Use a measuring tape or ruler to measure from the bottom edge of the hat to the shoulders. Add 1 inch (2.5 centimeters) to get the length of fabric needed for the back flap.

2 With the pencil make a mark on the hat in front of each ear. Take off the hat and measure between the marks. Add 1 inch (2.5 centimeters) to get the width of the back flap. Cut out a rectangle of fabric for the back flap, using the measurements above.

3 Make a hem on the sides and bottom by folding about 1/2 inch (1 centimeter) of fabric towards the inside of the flap (the part that will face your neck). Press the fold so there is a sharp crease. You can use an iron if an adult gives you permission. Squeeze out a thin wavy line of glue inside the fold to hold the hem flat. Let dry.

4 Glue the flap to the inside of the hat one side at a time. Lay the hat on its side on the newspaper. Along the bottom edge between the pencil mark and the back of the hat, squeeze out a thin wavy line of glue.

5 Hold the flap so that the hems are facing you. Attach the unhemmed top of the flap to the glue on the inside of the hat. Let dry. Repeat with the other side.

WORDS TO KNOW

kepi: a cap with a flat top and a flap down the back.

TECHNICAL CLOTHING FOR THE DESERT

Even in hot deserts, wearing shorts and a T-shirt is a bad idea. You'll lose too much water through sweat. You'll also expose your skin to the harsh rays of the sun.

Some experts recommend lightweight, quick-drying nylon shirts and pants. Others prefer breathable cotton—but cotton won't keep you warm at night or when it's wet. Wool is the fiber used in many traditional pieces of clothing in the desert because it's strong (if somewhat heavy) and warm at night.

Whichever you choose, just remember to pick long, loose-fitting clothing that will cover you, while trapping air between the cloth and your skin.

Temperature aside, the main reason for long, sturdy desert clothes is the sun. Our eyes can't see the sun's **ultraviolet (UV) radiation**, but it goes right through lightweight clothing to cause damage to living cells on and under the skin's surface. Without protection, you'll start to get a sunburn in about 15 minutes. Over time, too much UV exposure can also cause wrinkles, eye damage, and skin cancer.

You should always wear a hat in the desert. Choose one with a broad brim or a cloth in the back that will protect your face, ears, and neck. Sunglasses help too. They guard your eyes from damaging glare. Even in the shade, your eyes can get hit with UV radiation bouncing back from the desert floor.

WORDS TO KNOW

ultraviolet (UV) radiation: invisible sun rays that can damage the skin.

Ultraviolet Protection Factor (UPF): a rating number used to describe sun protection clothing.

Sun Protection Factor (SPF): a rating number used to describe sun protection skin lotion.

nomads: people who move from place to place.

FASCINATING FACT

Can rubber-bottomed shoes melt on desert pavement? Maybe. There have been reports of shoes melting during long running races through Death Valley, where the road can hit 200 degrees. So far, though, it's only an urban legend.

Australia, which has the highest rate of skin cancer in the world, has come up with a system to rate the UV protection of clothing. An **Ultraviolet Protection Factor (UPF)** rating of 20 means only 1/20 the amount of UV radiation can get through. A UPF rating of 15–39 is good, while 40 or above is excellent. High UPF ratings go to tightly woven, dark, heavy fabrics, as well as to loose-fitting shirts with long sleeves and high collars, and hats that shade the face, neck, and ears.

As for your feet, sturdy boots are the top recommendation for desert walking and hiking. They'll protect you from animals, plants, rocks, and the hot sand. And don't forget gaiters to keep the sand and grit out of your socks!

Any skin not covered by clothing should get a coating of sunscreen or sunblock. Sunscreen contains chemicals that absorb UV radiation. Sunblock reflects UV rays away from you. Pick one with a **Sun Protection Factor (SPF)** of at least 15.

SHELTER

You'll find very few towns or cities actually *in* the desert. Unless there's a perennial river or oasis that can provide water for raising animals or crops, it's just too hard to provide for a large population. And when rivers change their course or oases dry up, you're left with lost cities and ghost towns. So most permanent settlements are built on the desert's edge.

There are also desert people who live their lives as **nomads**. All their belongings—including the homes they live in—are portable. They can be bundled up and carried with them as they travel around. The earliest humans were nomads, but the number of people who live that way today is dwindling.

Those who do still live as nomads say they appreciate the sense of freedom their lifestyle gives them.

Permanent dwellings:

Deserts don't have many trees, so most ancient buildings were made of mud, clay, and stone rather than wood. The pyramids are one obvious example but other cultures created majestic stone structures as well.

The **Nabataeans** carved buildings right into the mountain walls in Petra, Jordan, on the edge of the Arabian Desert. Petra was a well-known trading center for over 400 years, but eventually the city was abandoned and forgotten. The ruins were "re-discovered" in 1812, and in 2007 Petra was voted one of the New Seven Wonders of the World.

Native Americans built some of their communities on high cliffs. In Mesa Verde, Colorado, the **Ancestral Puebloans** (also called the **Anasazi**) constructed roughly 600 cliff dwellings, probably so their enemies couldn't reach them. The largest, Cliff Palace, has 150 rooms and 75 open areas. It may have housed over 100 people at one time.

To see Cliff Palace today, you have to go up 120 uneven stone steps, and climb five, 8-foot (3-meter) ladders. The Balcony House tour is even more demanding. First you climb a 32-foot (10-meter) ladder. Then you crawl through a 12-foot-long (3.5-meter) tunnel. Finally, you scale a 60-foot (18-meter) open rock face via two, 10-foot (3-meter) ladders to exit the site. Mysteriously, Mesa Verde too was abandoned after a few generations.

WORDS TO KNOW

Nabataeans: people of an ancient Arab kingdom in present-day Jordan.

Ancestral Puebloan or Anasazi: member of a certain prehistoric Southwestern Native American tribe.

pueblo: a traditional Southwestern Native American community of attached adobe homes.

adobe: mud mixed with straw that's poured into forms or shaped into sun-dried bricks.

The Mesa Verde cliff dwellings were **pueblos**, or buildings made of **adobe**. There are pueblos in many parts of the southwest, and some are still used today. In fact, the oldest continuously inhabited community in the United States is a pueblo—the 1,000-year-old high rises in Taos Pueblo, New Mexico. When these were first built, the only way in or out of the individual apartments was an opening in the roof, but today there are doors and windows.

A similar technique was used to build the Great Mosque of Djenné in Mali, Africa.

Great Mosque of Djenné

The Great Mosque is the world's largest mud building. Its thick walls absorb heat during the day and release warmth at night. Wooden planks sticking out of the walls serve as decoration and as footholds for city residents who gather once a year to replaster the mosque. Another city of mud homes is Shibam, Yemen, on the Arabian Peninsula. Though dating to the sixteenth century, the buildings there look like modern apartment towers.

Modern buildings in the desert draw both on traditional designs and high technology. For instance, some new designs borrow the idea of buildings and homes built around open courtyards. Pools and gardens help keep the area cool.

— **FASCINATING FACT** —

Before moving to cliff dwellings, the people of Mesa Verde lived on top of the mesa in underground buildings.

Some architects have been inspired by ancient Iranian cooling towers. These towers have two sets of vents: one that faces the wind and draws cool air down into the house, and another that channels the hot air up and out. The architects have added large windows for solar heating in the winter.

Other new desert buildings turn their back on nature. They rely on air conditioning, not special designs, to keep cool. They also usually require large amounts of water pumped in to keep lawns green and swimming pools full. In Dubai on the Arabian Peninsula, artificial islands with huge housing complexes have been built. That kind of development puts a lot of pressure on the desert's resources, however, and is probably not a permanent solution for living in the desert.

— FASCINATING FACT —

Tepees, the type of cone-shaped tent used by Native Americans, were not common among desert tribes until the 1800s. When the United States government sent Native Americans to live on reservations, they replaced their buffalo hide tepees with ones manufactured from canvas.

TRY THIS: make a tent anchor

SUPPLIES

- 1 small square of cloth or plastic shopping bag for each tent anchor
- sand

Ever try to pitch a tent in loosely packed sand? It's hard to dig down far enough to keep your tent stakes in place. Here's a trick desert experts use.

1 Fill the bag or square of fabric with sand. If you're using fabric, fold the ends up to make a pouch. Tie the corners in a knot. Then tie them again.

2 Thread the tent lines between the knots in the fabric or through the handle of the plastic bag. Place the tent anchors far enough away from the tent to keep the lines tight.

3 When you're ready to break camp, just empty out your anchors and pack away for next time.

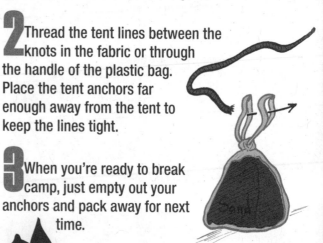

WORDS TO KNOW

tepee: a Native American cone-shaped tent, usually made of skins.

Bedouin: a nomadic Arab of the Arabian, Syrian, or North African deserts.

ger or **yurt:** a Central Asian round, domed tent.

lattice: a framework of crossed wood strips.

DESERT SHELTER ON THE MOVE

In the Arabian Desert, the **Bedouin** people are famous for their nomadic lifestyle. A tent is their mobile home. When it comes time to move, the tent is easily taken apart, rolled up, and packed on camels.

The traditional Bedouin tent is made of narrow strips of brown or black goats' hair wool, held up by poles. Each strip can be up to 25 feet (7 meters) long. The tent floor is open and covered with rugs. Inner "walls" of fabric divide the space into men's and women's sections, and cooking is done inside.

Another type of tent is the **ger**, also known as a **yurt**. This tent is used by Mongols in the Gobi Desert and by people in other parts of Central Asia. Like a Bedouin tent, a ger can be rolled up and transported by camel, yak, or truck.

A ger is a dome-shaped enclosure of white felt. The felt is made by beating and rolling wet sheep fleece. The walls are held up by a collapsible wooden **lattice** frame. And the supports that hold up the roof look like the spokes of a wheel, all connected to a small central hub at the top. Cooking is done on a stove in the center.

—**FASCINATING FACT**—

Gers or yurts made of modern materials have become popular in the United States as vacation cottages.

Modern camping tents are much smaller and lighter. Usually they're made of nylon or other high-tech fabrics. You probably won't need a pack animal to carry your tent, but you do need to pay attention to where you pitch it.

63

Before putting up your tent in the desert, experts advise that you make sure you're not in a dry riverbed. Also stay away from trails used by mountain lions or other big animals, and from loose rocks overhead. Avoid damp, dark corners where scorpions, spiders, or other creepy crawlies may be hiding. And once you've found the best spot, try to point the opening of your tent away from the sun and wind.

TRY THIS: BUILD AN UNDERGROUND DESERT SHADE SHELTER

SUPPLIES

- tarp, blanket, poncho, or other big piece of cloth
- 4 or more rocks or tent anchors (see page 62) to keep it in place

If you're stranded in the desert with no shade around, use the cool hours of the morning or evening to build a shade shelter. If possible, take a tip from animals like the desert tortoise and build your burrow underground. You can also practice this technique at the beach, in your yard, or indoors using sheets and pillows.

1 Find a spot between two dunes or rocks big enough to lie down in. Or dig a trench, piling up sand around three sides to make low walls.

2 Pull the cover over the opening and anchor it down flat.

3 For better insulation from the sun overhead, add a second layer. Take another cover and stretch it out on top of your anchors. Leave an air space between the two covers. Pile more anchors on top.

Tarp
Sand Anchor
2nd Tarp
Big Sandbox

HOW DESERT ANIMALS FIND FOOD

For you, drinking is more important than eating. (Remember the rule of three?) But for some desert animals, it's just the opposite. Animals like the addax— an endangered type of antelope from Africa—get all the fluids they need from grasses, shrubs, and succulents. There are even animals like the kangaroo rat that can make their own H_2O chemically as they digest dry seeds.

Many other desert animals survive because they can enjoy a wide variety of foods. A bird like the cactus wren of the Southwestern United States prefers insects, but it will also munch on lizards, frogs, cactus fruit, berries, and seeds. Coyotes will eat almost anything, including rodents, reptiles, and even scorpions and crickets.

FASCINATING FACT

Traditional Bedouin hospitality requires that any stranger be given food and shelter for three days.

With plants and animals so scarce, some desert animals have special adaptations that help them find things to eat. The great jerboa, a rodent with outsized ears, eyes, and feet, and a tuft of hair on the end of its tail, has long slender front claws it can use to comb through the sand to dig up seeds and insects. And the kangaroo's massive hind legs help it cover lots of ground as it hops about searching for vegetation, including grass, shrubs, and fungus.

Solar Cooking

Solar cooking is a modern but low-tech way to cook using the energy of the sun. It's a good choice in desert areas where firewood is hard to find and families can't afford oil for stoves. Solar cookers are also inexpensive, easy to make, and very portable. Even simple cardboard box cookers can reach 200-300 degrees Fahrenheit (94-149 degrees Celsius).

FASCINATING FACT

In central Africa, solar cookers given to war refugees save half a ton of wood a year each.

WHAT NATIVE DESERT PEOPLES EAT AND DRINK

Different cultures have developed their own strategies for obtaining food in the desert. **Foraging** for edible plants and animals is one of the most common. Cacti fruit like saguaro and prickly pears are a special treat. Amaranth leaves are used as an herb, and the seeds can be roasted or ground into flour. Lizards and snakes are boiled or fried. If you want to try some fresh-caught rattlesnake, be sure to cut off the head and bury it so no one accidentally steps on the **venom**-filled fangs!

Nomads often herd livestock, so their food travels with them. Sheep, goats, and camels can graze on land that's too dry for crops. When one area runs out of vegetation for grazing, the group moves on. Animals provide herdsmen with milk and meat, as well as wool, fur, and leather. Even the animals' **dung** is useful— i t can be burned for fuel!

In deserts where game animals live, native people hunt and trap. Kalahari San tribesmen track antelope with deadly bows and arrows tipped with poison made from beetle larvae, caterpillars, or snakes. They catch hares, guinea fowls, and other small animals in traps. In Australia, the boomerang was developed by the Aborigines for hunting.

Because there's so little rain, desert farming requires bringing water to the fields. Southwestern Native American farmers learned to use floodwater to irrigate crops such as beans, squash, corn, and chili peppers. In the Middle East, melon and cotton are grown using qanat-like irrigation systems or mechanized sprinklers. Meanwhile, Israeli farmers are beginning to use

WORDS TO KNOW

foraging: collecting food that grows wild.

venom: poison injected by animals through biting or stinging.

venomous: poisonous fluid injected by an animal.

dung: animal poop.

labneh: soft, strained, yogurt cheese.

pita bread: a thin, flat, sometimes hollow, round loaf of bread.

tortilla: a thin, round piece of cornmeal bread.

TRY THIS: make YOGURT CHEESE

SUPPLIES

- one cup plain yogurt
- salt
- strainer
- coffee filters or paper towels
- medium bowl

Labneh, or yogurt cheese spread, is easy to make from ordinary yogurt and stays fresh even longer. It tastes a little like cream cheese. This cheese is popular throughout the Middle East for breakfast, in sandwiches, and as an appetizer. It is often served on pita bread with olive oil, tomatoes, olives, cucumbers, or mint.

coffee filter strainer

1 Stir a pinch of salt into the yogurt. Line the strainer with the coffee filter. Place it in the bowl.

Yogurt

2 Pour the yogurt into the strainer. Cover with another filter. Place the bowl in the refrigerator overnight to drain.

3 It's ready to eat the next day! Spread on bread or crackers. To store, move the labneh to an air-tight container.

recycled sewer water on their tomatoes and peppers. But population growth and global warming make large-scale desert farming a risky business.

COOKING AND EATING

Even if you've never been to the desert, you've probably enjoyed some desert food without realizing it. **Pita bread** you use for pocket sandwiches is a staple through-out the Middle East. It's especially convenient for nomadic people, because it can be made over an open fire on special dome-shaped metal pans.

Tortillas are popular throughout the American Southwestern desert. Traditionally they were made by soaking corn kernels to remove their skins.

WORDS TO KNOW

arthritis: a painful bone condition that can cause swelling in the joints.

yogurt: milk that has been thickened by special bacteria.

preservative: something that protects against spoiling.

After grinding the corn into cornmeal, women made a dough, rolled the tortillas out, and baked them on a flat griddle. Grinding the corn kernels was hard work. The skeletons of many Ancestral Puebloan women show signs of **arthritis**, which some archaeologists believe was caused by spending hours grinding corn with stone tools.

Yogurt originally came from Central Asia and spread to the Middle East. It is made by adding special kinds of bacteria to the milk of cows, goats, or other animals. The bacteria produce lactic acid, which makes the milk thick and slightly sour. It also acts as a **preservative**. That made yogurt useful for people who relied on milk as a major food source in a hot climate.

TRY THIS: reflective cup cooker challenge

Solar cookers work by concentrating the rays of the sun. Most types of solar cookers use shiny surfaces that reflect the rays where they're needed. Many cookers are black inside, because black surfaces absorb light and release it as heat. Black cooking pots are also used for the same reason. And some kinds have a clear cover to help hold in the heat. Use these ideas to design some simple solar cookers and see which works best.

SUPPLIES

- paper or Styrofoam hot drink cups
- black construction paper
- aluminum foil
- Mylar film (the shiny inside of snack food bags)
- piece of chocolate
- sunny spot

1 Make your test cups by covering them, inside or out, with the different materials. You can also add layers of insulation, or try cups made of metal or glass. Also try using a plain cup for comparison.

2 Place a piece of chocolate in each cup. See how long each cup takes to melt the chocolate. Which is the most efficient? When you're done, go ahead and taste the test results!

SOLAR HEAT RAYS

ALUMINUM FOIL

CONCENTRATED HEAT

SOLAR COOKER

PIECE OF CHOCOLATE

CHAPTER 6

Desert Dangers and How to Avoid Them

here are other hazards in the desert besides thirst, heat, and cold. Desert explorers need to know how to find their way, how to deal with sand and wind, which plants and animals might be dangerous, and how to avoid getting sick. You'll also need to know where the possibility of trouble from desert people might come from. Your desert journey will be much more enjoyable if you are prepared.

GPS?

DESERT PLANT GUIDE?

Aloe Vera?

CHECK.

CHECK.

DOUBLE-CHECK.

FINDING YOUR WAY WITHOUT ROADS OR LANDMARKS

It's easy to get lost in the desert. There are vast distances to cover, and few landmarks, people, or towns. In many places you won't even have a paved road to travel on. But there are a few **navigation** tricks, both ancient and modern, that will help you find your way.

For instance, one way to get your bearings in a sandy desert is to know from which direction the prevailing winds usually blow. You can then tell where the wind is coming from by the shape of the surrounding dunes. You can also look for ancient trails on the desert floor. And be alert to clues like the California compass barrel cactus. It got its name by leaning towards the south, into the sun.

Judging distance is a tough skill in the desert. The air is so clear that objects seem closer than they really are. Some experts suggest figuring that the object you're headed towards is really three times as far away as it looks.

One way to estimate how far you've already gone is to practice counting the steps you take. You'll need

OH! NOW I KNOW WHERE I AM!
Polarized Light

to know how much ground you typically cover in 10 steps. A grown man usually goes 25 feet, or roughly 8 meters, in 10 steps.

Trying to use a map in the desert has its own special twists. In large flat areas there may not be any landmarks to go by. Rivers drawn on a map may have moved or dried up. A trail climbing up and down a winding

WORDS TO KNOW

navigation: the science of getting from place to place.

polarized: light waves that vibrate in one direction.

GPS: stands for Global Positioning System, which can locate its position using signals from satellites above the earth.

─ FASCINATING FACT ─

Scientists have recently discovered that the desert ant has specialized eyes that act like a built-in compass. Its eyes are able to detect **polarized** light, which moves in one particular direction. So even if it can't see the sun or any landmarks, the desert ant can figure out which way it's going.

canyon with steep vertical walls is hard to pick out on a two-dimensional map. A compass can tell you which direction to go in, but figuring out how long it's going to take you to get there can be a puzzle.

Many desert explorers find **GPS** devices extremely handy. With a GPS, no other information, not even a map, is needed. A GPS uses signals from four or more satellites orbiting in space to pinpoint its location on Earth. Some types of GPS are accurate enough to tell where you are within an arm's length.

TRY THIS: FINDING DIRECTION USING THE SHADOW-TIP METHOD

Here's an easy way to figure out direction without a compass. It's great for the desert, but you can use it anyplace the sun is shining.

SUPPLIES
- a stick
- 2 small stones
- a sunny spot

1 Find someplace flat and set the stick upright in the ground. Mark the tip of its shadow with the stone.

2 Wait 15 minutes, until the shadow tip has moved. Mark the new location with another stone.

3 Now draw a line from the first stone to the second. Since the sun moves from east to west across the sky, its shadow moves west to east. So the first point is west, and the second point is east.

4 If you stand looking west along your line and stick out your arms, your right hand will point north, and your left hand will point south.

1st Mark: WEST
2nd Mark: EAST

WORDS TO KNOW

latitude: distance north or south of the equator, measured in degrees.

issabah: Arabic word meaning the width of a finger.

kamal: Arabic navigational tool.

Like any piece of electronic equipment, a GPS can malfunction, run out of power, or be damaged by sand, wind, or rain. So it's good to know a few low-tech methods of navigation too.

Navigating by the stars makes a lot of sense in the broiling hot deserts of the Middle East. That's because it's cooler to travel at night. Ancient Arab travelers developed a quick method of using their fingers to determine their **latitude** by measuring the distance between the horizon and the North Star. The further north you go, the higher the North Star appears in the sky. At the equator it sits on the horizon, and at the North Pole, it appears directly overhead. So measuring the distance between the horizon and the North Star in the sky tells you what latitude you're at on the earth.

To measure the height of the North Star, ancient travelers would hold one arm out straight in front of them, and bend their hand so that their fingers lined up with the horizon. Then they would see how many fingers fit between the horizon and the North Star. One finger width was called an **issabah**. Obviously, this method worked best if you were no more than eight finger-widths away from the equator!

The **kamal** was a navigational tool that could be used instead of fingers. It consisted of a wooden rectangle with a hole in the middle of it and a string going through the hole. Instead of measuring the distance between the horizon and the North Star in finger widths, it was measured by the width of the kamal.

—FASCINATING FACT—

The desert is a great place for star gazing because of its clear skies and distance from city lights. In fact, the world's most advanced optical instrument, the European Southern Observatory's Very Large Telescope, is located in the Atacama Desert of Chile.

The higher the North Star appeared in the sky, the closer the user had to hold the kamal to his eye. The distance from the kamal to the user's eye was measured by the string. Actually, the string measured the distance to the user's teeth, because that is how the user held it! To record the latitude of a particular place, the traveler would tie a knot in the string where he was holding it in his teeth. Whenever he put that knot in his teeth and the horizon and North Star were lined up with the kamal, he would know what latitude he was at. Another way to use the kamal was to tie knots in the string marking off each issabah of distance between the horizon and the North Star. The kamal is still used today by sea kayakers for estimating the distance to land.

TRY THIS: make a kamal

SUPPLIES

- index card or other rectangular piece of cardboard
- pencil
- string (about one arm's length)
- a clear night

The further away you are from the equator, the bigger your kamal rectangle needs to be. If you live at a latitude where the North Star is very high in the sky, tie your string around a ruler or long stick instead.

1 With the pencil, punch a hole in the middle of your cardboard rectangle. Take the string and put it through the hole. Tie knots on both sides of the card so it doesn't come off.

2 Go outside after dark. To find the North Star, look for the Big Dipper. It looks like a square made up of four stars with a handle made up of three stars. Follow the two stars on the outside of the dipper's bowl upward. They point to the North Star.

3 Hold the bottom of the cardboard or stick even with the horizon and the top so that it touches the North Star. Pull the string toward your face. (If you want to be authentic, hold it in your teeth!) Where the string touches your face, tie a knot. This is a marker that will always show you when you are at your home latitude.

4 Next time you travel north or south, take out your kamal and mark your new location on your string with another knot. Your kamal can be a record of the different latitudes you've visited.

WORDS TO KNOW

sandstorm: clouds of sand blown along the surface by high winds.

dust storm: clouds of dust blown into the atmosphere by high winds.

blood rain: rain colored by red dust particles.

whirlwind: a rotating column of air that moves across the ground.

dust devil: a whirlwind that has picked up dirt and debris.

SAND HAZARD

Sand might seem harmless, but it can cause a lot of problems. Sand can get into your shoes, clothes, packs, and shelter. It can get in your food and drink and leave you with a permanent sandy taste in your mouth. Sand blown in your eyes can cause damage and even blindness. It wears away at everything, including clothing and equipment. Glass becomes scratched and frosted, and gears and electronic circuits get stopped up. Blowing sand creates static electricity that can even knock out computer systems and radio transmissions.

Sandstorms and **dust storms** can arrive suddenly and cause serious problems for the desert explorer. From a distance you will see a solid wall of dust and debris, often miles long and several thousand feet high. When it hits, it blots out the sun and cuts visibility to zero. Most sandstorms only last a few minutes. Dust storms, on the other hand, can build higher, last longer, and travel farther—even across oceans to other continents. If you're caught in blowing sand and can't get to shelter, mark the direction you're traveling in. Then wet a cloth to cover your face, lie down, and wait it out.

Desert winds can also cause other unusual phenomena. **Blood rain** is the gruesome name given to a mixture of red sand and precipitation that sometimes falls in Europe.

It's caused by dust from the Sahara that's picked up and carried by the wind across the Mediterranean Sea and the Atlantic Ocean.

Whirlwinds are spinning columns of air that spring up out of nowhere and start moving across the ground. When they pick up dirt and debris and become visible, they're called **dust devils**. They occur on calm days when the ground heats up, making the air on the surface warmer than the air above. Hot air is lighter than cool air, and sometimes it begins rising in a column. Then, if the hot air makes a slight movement sideways up above it can set the column turning. Whirlwinds and dust devils can range from 500 to 1,000 feet (150 to 300 meters) or more in height and spin as fast as 60 miles (96 kilometers) an hour. While they usually disappear as quickly as they appear, some go on for hours.

——FASCINATING FACT——

Central and South American rainforests get most of their mineral nutrients from dust blown over from the Sahara Desert. Dust storms also deposit much-needed iron in the ocean. They even improve the growth of the tropical fruit plantain in Hawaii!

Desert Quicksand

You may have watched exciting scenes of people or animals sinking into pits of dry quicksand in movies. But experts say dry quicksand exists only in the laboratory. In the desert, quicksand is usually found along sandy riverbanks. It looks solid—until you step in it—but it is really a thick soup of sand and water. If you get caught in quicksand, don't flail around. Try to lie flat and "swim" across the sand to firmer ground. You can help someone caught in quicksand by throwing a rope or holding out a stick for them to grab. Then pull them to safety.

DANGEROUS WEATHER

Did you know that more people drown in the desert than die of thirst? That's because violent rainstorms cause flash flooding.

Flash floods can catch hikers and other vacationers so quickly they don't have time to escape. They occur when rain far from the desert collects and fills narrow, dry riverbeds. In 2002, the Pollard family was lucky to survive what park rangers told them was a once-in-a-century flood in Canyonlands National Park, Utah.

WORDS TO KNOW

hail: precipitation in the form of small balls of ice and snow.

fulgurite: a glassy tube formed when lightning strikes sand.

Art and Mihoko Pollard, along with their two small children, were in their off-road vehicle driving on a park road that followed a dry streambed. Suddenly they saw a 4-inch curb of water coming at them. The water quickly rose halfway up their windshield, picked up their vehicle and carried it 4 miles (6.5 kilometers) downstream. The parents managed to climb out with the kids and float to shore. No one was injured, but the vehicle lost a wheel, flipped over, and ended up buried halfway in mud.

You also have to watch out for cold fronts that can lower the temperature as much as 50 degrees in a matter of seconds. Rain can sometimes turn into **hail**, which can be soft and sticky and freeze your skin. In those conditions, it's extra important to have clothes that can keep you warm, even when wet.

Desert Glass

When lightning strikes sand, it occasionally leaves a souvenir called a **fulgurite**. These hollow tubes of glass are created when the intense heat of the lightning bolt fuses quartz sand crystals together. Fulgurites are common in the Great Sand Dunes National Park in Colorado.

Other major shocks can have the same effect. Libyan desert glass in northern Africa is believed to be the result of a meteorite crash landing. And rare Trinitite glass was created when a nuclear bomb went off at the Trinity test site in New Mexico during World War II.

Lightning is also a risk in areas where you may be the tallest thing around. The electricity of a lightning strike travels along the easiest path to the ground—and you don't want that easy path to be your body!

If you're caught out in the open during a lightning storm with no shelter, go into what safety experts call the "lightning position." The goal is to make yourself as small and low as possible and keep contact with the ground to a minimum. Drop anything metal and crouch down into a ball with your feet together. Hold onto your knees or cover your ears with your hands. If you have a sleeping pad or soft backpack, crouch on it for more insulation from electricity on the ground.

PLANTS TO AVOID

Cactus spines, or needles, aren't poisonous, but they can be annoying and painful. If you get stuck with one, you'll have to remove it so the wound doesn't become infected. Usually you can pull out a cactus spine like you would a splinter. They can be tricky, though, because some cactus spines have little hooks on the end to hold fast. Ouch!

One cactus, the jumping cholla, doesn't really jump out at you, but it may seem like it. If you brush up against one, an entire segment will break off and attach itself to your clothing or skin. Don't use your hands to pry it off! Instead, use a fork, comb, or stick. You may need scissors or pliers to cut through the stubborn barbed quills.

Some desert plants, such as jimson weed, are poisonous if you eat them. Never taste a desert plant unless you can identify it as being edible.

CAREFUL! THEY BITE!

Desert animals can be much scarier than desert plants. You probably won't see a lot of them. Most desert denizens nap the day away under rocks, in underground burrows, or in damp, shady crevices. It's in the mornings, the evenings, and after dark that you have to watch out for dangerous creatures. While a sting or bite from a desert animal can really hurt, few are deadly to humans.

Desert experts from the Southwest will tell you that it's rare to come across a Gila monster. If you do, it's best to admire them from a safe distance. Named after the Gila (pronounced "he-lah") River in Arizona, Gila monsters (and their cousins, Mexican beaded lizards) are the biggest lizards in North America. They're also the only venomous lizards in the world. But scientists believe that Gila monsters use their venom mainly to protect themselves. Most of the animals they hunt for food, such as baby birds and worms, are small enough to kill with just a bite from the Gila monster's powerful jaws.

Luckily for their helpless prey, Gila monsters have big chunky tails to store fat in, so they don't move too fast. Gila monsters are protected by law. They are becoming rarer as human development cuts into their habitat.

You might hear a rattlesnake before you see it. That's because they come with their own warning system. The rattles on the end of their tails are made of **keratin**, the same stuff fingernails are made of. Shaking the rattles creates a hissing sound that keeps bigger animals away. The rattler doesn't always sound the alarm, though, so you still need to keep your eyes open.

WORDS TO KNOW

keratin: protein that makes up hair and nails.

arachnid: class of animals including spiders and scorpions with two body segments and four pairs of legs.

pincer: a claw with two points that can pinch together.

Death Adder

─FASCINATING FACT─

Be careful even with a dead rattler. The snake's nervous system can still trigger it to strike and inject venom after it has died.

Rattlesnakes are just one of the venomous snakes you may encounter in the desert. Cobras live around the edge of the Sahara Desert and in Arabia. They are known for rearing up and spreading out a hood of skin to look even more fearsome. And the desert death adder from Australia is one of the most venomous land snakes in the world. It has a big flabby body that thins down to a skinny tail tip, which it uses like bait to lure prey in.

Snake venom can cause internal bleeding or paralyze your heart and lungs, so a snake bite always needs to be taken seriously.

Did you know that scorpions are **arachnids**, or members of the spider family? That means they have eight legs and two main body parts. What makes scorpions different is their front **pincers** and their stinger.

The pincers look like arms with claws on the end, but they're really very elaborate mouth parts. The stinger is not a tail but the hind end of their body. It curls up and over the scorpion's back, ready to defend it from attack. All scorpions are venomous, but most scorpion stings are no more dangerous to human beings than bee stings. Others, like the Sonoran bark scorpion, can cause numbness, frothing at the mouth, breathing problems, and twitching.

Speaking of spiders, the tarantula is a big one, but it's not venomous—at least not to us. Like most desert spiders, it lives in a burrow, not a web. Instead of waiting for a victim to come along, the tarantula chases down and kills beetles, grasshoppers, small lizards, and mice. It does this by injecting venom through its fangs.

> **—FASCINATING FACT—**
> Scorpions are found all over the world and in many different environments. You can even find them in the Himalayas, 12,000 feet up!

Camel Spider

Camel spiders are also big and hairy, but not as dangerous as they look. In fact, they're not really spiders, but a relative called a **solifugid**. They eat insects, rodents, lizards, snakes, and small birds by crushing them to a pulp with their pincers. Then they liquefy them with chemicals and suck up the remains.

WORDS TO KNOW

solifugid: animal related to spiders and scorpions.

succulent: a type of plant with spongy tissue that holds moisture.

FASCINATING FACT

Camel spiders can grow as large as 6 inches (15 centimeters) long. The hairy bug's name comes from the camel-like hump on its back.

TRY THIS: aloe vera for healing and moisturizing

Aloe vera, a **succulent** from North Africa with long spiky leaves growing out of its base, is a popular houseplant. Doctors have also found that it has anti-inflammatory and wound-healing properties that fight bacteria, virus, and fungus infections. Cosmetic companies add aloe vera gel to make-up, tissues, moisturizers, soaps, sunscreens, and shampoos. And many people use it at home to treat cuts, burns, and rashes.

SUPPLIES

• a well-watered aloe vera houseplant

1 Get permission to cut or break off a leaf from an aloe plant. Watch out for the little teeth along the edge.

2 Gel will start to ooze out of the break in the leaf. Test a very small amount on your skin. (Ask an adult first, since aloe can sting some people's skin.) If it feels soothing, rub a little wherever your skin is rough or itchy. Avoid your eyes and mouth. Although it's good for mouth sores, it tastes terrible!

Desert Medicine

People have been using desert plant, animal, and other organic products as medicine since prehistoric times. One of the oldest grave sites ever found, built by early humans in the Iraqi desert, included the remains of several kinds of medicinal flowers that were important to them. One of them was a woody shrub called ephedra. Ephedra contains a substance used in cold medicines to clear the breathing passages. It's also a **stimulant** that speeds up the heart rate.

WORDS TO KNOW

stimulant: a drug that increases a body function such as the heart rate.

capsaicin: the chemical that makes hot peppers feel hot.

Southwestern Native Americans used the creosote bush for diarrhea, colds, and kidney pain. A drug to help diabetes patients known as "lizard spit" was developed in 2005 from Gila monster saliva. And **capsaicin**, the spicy chemical in cayenne pepper, is used for thinning blood and soothing stomach ulcers. In the Israeli desert, researchers are finding ways to use chemicals in red algae to fight disease and to use as sunscreen.

Tips for Traveling Where Dangerous Creatures are Found

- Don't play host to unwanted guests. Shake out all your belongings—including clothes, boots, packs, tents, and sleeping bags—every time you use them.

- Critters like to hide in ruins, villages, garbage dumps, caves, and natural rock outcroppings that offer shade. Make sure you look before you step, sit, or climb.

- If you come upon a worrisome beast out on the trail, observe it from a safe distance. Don't mess with it, and it probably won't mess with you!

- If you're bitten or stung by any desert animal, clean the wound and get medical help as soon as you can. Chances are all you'll just need is some pain relievers and a cold compress, but it's wise to get expert advice, just in case.

TRAVELERS' ADVISORY

Deserts have been the site of wars and conflicts since the beginning of recorded time. First Romans, then Crusaders, and then Napoleon swept down from Europe to the Middle East. Genghis Khan and his Mongol hordes used their skill as horsemen to control the Gobi Desert and conquer China. And in World War II, German Field Marshal Erwin Rommel was known as "The Desert Fox" for his success in invading North Africa.

Sadly, wars and violence are still the rule in many deserts around the world today. A 2008 list of "The World's Worst Holiday Spots" included the African republics of Sierra Leone and Niger and the central Asian countries of Iraq and Afghanistan. So be sure to research any desert destinations before you go.

Lawrence of Arabia

One of the most famous desert war- and peace-makers of all time was Lawrence of Arabia. His real name was T.E. Lawrence and he was an English archaeologist who worked in the Middle East in the early 1900s. At the time, the Arab world was controlled by Europe and the Ottoman Empire in Turkey.

When World War I broke out, Lawrence joined the British Army in Cairo, Egypt. In 1916, he helped lead the Great Arab Revolt against the Turks. Newspapers printed photos of Lawrence in his Arab robes and made him famous. A few years later he helped the British give Arab countries their independence. The classic 1962 movie *Lawrence of Arabia*, which includes many striking scenes of desert sand dunes and stony fields, is based on his story.

SHOW RESPECT FOR THE DESERT

The biggest threat in the desert isn't from the sun, heat, or sand. It's from human beings, and what they may be doing to the desert. As cities and farms expand into and around the desert, so does the demand for desert resources such as oil, water, and land.

WORDS TO KNOW

desertification: the change from grassland to desert-like conditions.

In places like Central Asia, the Southwestern United States, and the Middle East, human development is bumping up against the habitat of animals like bighorn sheep and desert tortoises. The Asian houbara bustard, a large bird popular in the Arab world for its meat, is threatened by hunting as well as by human settlements moving into its territory. These developments need more and more water. Underground aquifers, which took millions of years to fill, are being drained so fast they'll be used up in only a few decades. Any water that's left becomes too salty. Meanwhile, rivers that are diverted to desert settlements take away water from the desert plants and animals that need it.

"Dust Bowl"

Outside the desert, in the semi-arid margins, another threat is at work— **desertification**. This is when semi-arid areas begin to dry up and die. Global warming, which is making some parts of the world hotter and dryer, is partly to blame. But so are overgrazing, too much farming, and excessive wood gathering.

Entire regions have been destroyed by desertification. In the United States, a terrible drought in the 1930s turned farmland in the Great Plains into a "Dust Bowl." Millions of families lost their farms and were forced to find jobs in other parts of the country.

In the 1960s, the former Soviet Union took water from the Aral Sea in Kazakhstan for nearby farms. The sea began to shrink, and fishing towns found themselves suddenly far from the water's edge. Today the Aral Sea is half its original size, and both people and animals have gone.

If you're one of the millions of people who visit the desert each year, you could

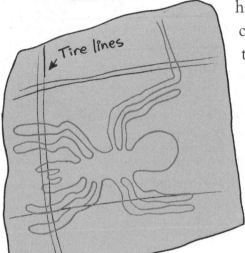

Tire lines

have an effect too—a big one. When you damage a cactus or "bust the crust," it takes decades for that life to grow back. Hiking, mountain biking, or driving an off-road vehicle outside of designated trails creates permanent marks in the desert floor. For example, satellite photographs show tire tracks crossing the Nazca drawings in Chile that were created thousands of years ago. Those ancient works of art can never be repaired or replaced.

Luckily, there are some ways to fix this fragile environment. You can help save the desert and the lands around it by using water and other resources wisely.

You can support the preservation and restoration of native trees and plants, which help keep desert soils from drying up and blowing away. And when you visit the desert, choose activities that make the least possible impact on the land. Be sure to always follow the rules put in place to protect the environment.

The desert may look bleak and empty, but as you've learned, it's home to countless species. From the tiny darkling beetle collecting fog along the ridges on its back, to the giant saguaro cactus with its trunk that expands after a rain, every inhabitant of the desert has adapted to life in a dry and rugged climate. That includes the 500 million people who live in or around the world's deserts. They've learned to appreciate every drop of fresh water ... and you should too! By helping desert life to thrive, you're helping to preserve life throughout the planet.

GLOSSARY

adobe: mud mixed with straw shaped into sun-dried bricks.

algae: small, plant-like organism.

Ancestral Puebloan or Anasazi: member of a certain prehistoric Southwestern Native American tribe.

aquifer: an absorbent layer of rock, sand, or gravel that carries water underground.

arachnid: class of animals including spiders and scorpions with two body segments and four pairs of legs.

archaeologist: a scientist who studies ancient people and their cultures.

arid: extremely dry.

artesian aquifer: an aquifer squeezed between two waterproof layers, putting the water under high pressure.

arthritis: a painful bone condition that can cause swelling in the joints.

avalanche: sand, rock, snow, or other material moving quickly down a mountainside.

barchan: a moving, crescent-shaped sand dune.

Bedouin: a nomadic Arab.

biological soil crust: small, highly specialized organisms that form a skin on the desert surface.

biome: a large natural area with a distinctive climate, geology, water resources, and plants and animals that are adapted for life there.

blood rain: rain colored by red dust.

breechcloth: a cloth worn about the waist as clothing in warm climates.

butte: a flat-topped stone column.

canyon: a deep, narrow valley with steep sides carved by flowing water.

caravan: travelers leading a train of pack animals through the desert.

carbon dioxide: a gas that can trap the sun's heat in the air, produced by breathing, by rotting dead matter, and by burning fossil fuels like oil and coal.

chlorophyll: a green coloring found in plants, which helps absorb light energy for photosynthesis.

climate: the long-term average weather pattern of a region.

clone: an organism that is genetically identical to its parent.

concentrated: a lot of one substance in a mixture.

condense: change from a gas into a solid

corrode: to eat away at metal gradually by chemical action.

crustacean: an aquatic animal like a shrimp or crab with a hard outer shell.

dehydration: the unhealthy loss of fluid in the body.

del: long, loose jacket worn in Mongolia.

density: the amount of a material there is in a particular amount of space.

desalination: removing the salt.

desert: a place that gets less than 10 inches of rain a year.

desertification: the change from grassland to desert.

desert pavement, reg, gibber, gobi: a thin surface layer of closely packed pebbles.

desert varnish: a dark coating produced by bacteria on desert rocks.

drought: a long period of dry weather that affects living things in an environment.

dune: a hill or ridge of sand piled up by the wind.

dung: animal poop.

dust devil: a whirlwind that has picked up dirt and debris.

dust storm: clouds of dust blown by high winds.

elevation: distance above or below sea level.

ephemeral: lasting a very short time.

erg: Arabic for sea of sand.

erosion: worn away by wind or water.

estivate: when the body slows down during hot weather.

ethnic: a group whose members share a similar culture.

evaporation: when liquid water is converted into vapor by the sun or other heat source.

forage: collect wild food.

fossil: rocks with the remains or imprint of prehistoric life.

fulgurite: a glassy tube formed when lightning strikes sand.

gaiters: cloth shoe coverings that reach up to the knee.

ger or yurt: a Central Asian round, domed tent.

geothermal: heated by the earth's inner core.

global warming: climate change that causes the average temperature of the air and oceans to rise.

GPS: Global Positioning System, which can locate its position using signals from satellites above the earth.

Hadley cell: currents of air moving over the subtropic and tropic zones.

hail: precipitation in the form of small balls of ice and snow.

hajj: a religious journey Muslims make to Mecca in present-day Saudi Arabia.

horizon: where the earth and the sky meet in a landscape.

humidity: the amount of water vapor present in the air.

Ice Age: a period of time when a large portion of the earth's surface was covered by ice.

85

Glossary

irrigation: bringing water to a dry area to help grow crops.

kaffiyeh: an Arab cloth head covering.

kamal: Arabic navigational tool.

kepi: a cap with a flat top and a flap down the back.

keratin: protein that makes up hair and nails

labneh: soft yogurt cheese.

latitude: distance north or south of the equator, measured in degrees.

lattice: a framework of crossed wood strips.

leeward: side facing away from the wind.

lichen: a combination of fungus and algae.

linear dunes: sand dunes forming regular lines.

mesa: a separated section of a plateau.

meteorite: a rocky or metallic object from space which lands on the earth.

mirage: an optical effect that looks like a pool of water, caused by bending light rays.

molten: made liquid by heat.

mosque: a building where Muslims gather to worship.

Nabataeans: people of an ancient Arab kingdom in present-day Jordan.

navigation: the science of getting from place to place.

nomads: people who move from place to place.

oasis: a green, fertile area surrounded by desert.

paleontologist: a scientist who studies fossils.

parabolic: crescent-shaped dunes that form because plants grow on their arms, holding them in place as the dunes are pushed forward by the wind.

perennial: present throughout the whole year.

photosynthesis: a process in plants in which carbon dioxide gas from the air combines with water and light energy to make sugars for food.

pilgrim: someone making a religious journey to a holy site.

pincer: a claw with two points that can pinch together.

pita bread: a thin, flat bread.

plateau: a flat, high area.

playa: a dry lake bed with a hard, flat, clay bottom.

polarized: light waves that vibrate in one direction.

pothole: small, temporary desert pool.

precipitation: all forms of wet weather, including rain, snow, sleet, and hail.

preservative: something that protects against spoiling.

prevailing wind: wind that blows mostly from one direction.

pueblo: a traditional Southwestern Native American community of attached adobe homes.

qanat: an underground water canal.

radiate: send out energy.

reservoir: an artificial lake used for collecting water.

salinity: the amount of salt in a mixture.

saltation: jumping.

sandstorm: clouds of sand blown along the surface by high winds.

semiarid: getting 10–20 inches (25–50 centimeters) of precipitation a year.

shaman: a spiritual leader trained in a group's traditions and healing rituals.

Silk Road: an ancient trade route between China and the Mediterranean.

solifugid: animal related to spiders and scorpions.

spring: water from underground.

star dune: a sand dune with a high center and three or more arms coming out from it.

stomata: a tiny pore in a plant that can be opened or closed to let air pass through.

strewn field: an area where meteorites have fallen.

subtropics: the region of the earth to the north and south of the tropics.

succulent: a type of plant with spongy tissue that holds moisture.

Sun Protection Factor (SPF): a rating number used to describe sun protection skin lotion.

tortilla: a thin, round piece of cornmeal bread.

traditional: old way of doing things.

transpiration: when a plant loses water vapor through the openings in its leaves or stem.

traverse: a zigzag way up or down a steep hill.

tropics: the region of the earth around the equator.

ultraviolet (UV) radiation: invisible sun rays that can damage skin.

Ultraviolet Protection Factor (UPF): a rating number used to describe sun protection clothing.

venom: poison injected by animals through biting or stinging.

wadi, arroyo: dry channel cut by water.

Western Hemisphere: the half of the earth that includes North and South America.

whirlwind: a rotating column of air that moves across the ground.

windward: side facing the wind.

yardang: a ridge of rock shaped by wind.

yogurt: milk that has been thickened by special bacteria.

RESOURCES

⟞⟞⟐⟝⟝ BOOKS ⟞⟞⟐⟝⟝

Allaby, Michael. *Deserts.* Chelsea House, 2006.

Annerino, John. *Desert Survivor: An Adventurer's Guide to Exploing the Great American Desert.* Four Walls Eight Windows, 2001.

Brown, John. *Journey Into the Desert.* Oxford University Press, 2002.

Castaldo, Nancy F. *Deserts: An Activity Guide for Ages 6-9.* Chicago Review Press, 2004.

Davenport, Gregory J. *Surviving the Desert.* Stackpole Books, 2004.

Flegg, Jim. *Deserts: Miracle of Life.* Facts on File, 1993.

Guiberson, Brenda Z. *Cactus Hotel.* H. Holt, 1991.

Harris, Nathaniel. *Atlas of the World's Deserts.* Fitzroy Dearborn, 2003.

Jenkins, Martin. *Deserts.* Lerner Publications, 1995.

Lazaroff, David Wentworth. *Arizona-Sonora Desert Museum Book of Answers.* Arizona-Sonora Desert Museum Press, 1998.

Le Rochais, Marie-Ange. *Desert Trek: An Eye-Opening Journey Through the World's Driest Places.* Walker & Co., 2001.

Pipe, Jim. *Desert Survival.* Gareth Stevens Pub., 2008.

Reynolds, Jan. *Sahara: Vanishing Cultures.* Harcourt Brace Jovanovich, 1991.

Rozario, Paul. *Spreading Deserts.* Raintree, 2004.

Silver, Donald M. *Cactus Desert.* W. H. Freeman, 1995.

Simon, Seymour. *Deserts.* Morrow Junior Books, 1990.

Stilwell, Alexander. *The Encyclopedia of Survival Techniques.* The Lyons Press, 2000.

Storm, Rory. *Desert Survivor's Guide.* Scholastic, 2001.

Warren, Andres and Tony Allan. *Guide to Deserts.* Firefly Books Inc., 2006.

⟞⟞⟐⟝⟝ WEB SITES ⟞⟞⟐⟝⟝

Deserts of the World

California Academy of Sciences: The Great Sahara Desert
www.calacademy.org/exhibits/africa/exhibit/sahara

Deserts: Geology and Resources by Alta Sharon Walker (US Geological Survey)
http://pubs.usgs.gov/gip/deserts

Living Desert, Palm Desert, CA
www.livingdesert.org

Missouri Botanical Garden Biomes of the World: Desert www.mbgnet.net/sets/desert

My Triops www.mytriops.com

National Geographic Deserts Information
http://environment.nationalgeographic.com/environment/habitats/desert-profile.html

Saudi Aramco World Magazine
www.saudiaramcoworld.com

United Nations Environment Program: Global Deserts Outlook www.unep.org/geo/gdoutlook

Deserts of the United States

Arizona-Sonora Desert Museum
www.desertmuseum.org

Desert Survivors (University of Nevada, Las Vegas)
http://sciences.unlv.edu/desertsurvivors

Desert USA
www.desertusa.com

USGS Death Valley National Park Virtual FieldTrip
http://geomaps.wr.usgs.gov/parks/deva

Utah Geological Survey http://geology.utah.gov

RESOURCES

Desert Travel and Recreation

California Deserts Visitors Association
www.californiadeserts.org

The Cultured Traveler (February 2006 issue)
www.crossculturedtraveler.com/archives/
FEB2006/Lead_Story.htm

Dreamride Mountain Bike Skills
www.dreamride.com/skillsindex.html

United Nations World Tourism Organization:
Sustainable Development of Ecotourism in
Desert Areas,
www.world-tourism.org/sustainable/IYE/
Regional_Activites/Algeria/Algeria

Utah Travel
www.utah.com

Desert Survival

Australian Radiation Protection and Nuclear Safety
Agency Clothing and Solar UV Protection
www.arpansa.gov.au/RadiationProtection/Fact-
sheets/is_UVProtection.cfm

Discovery Survival Zone: Desert
http://dsc.discovery.com/survival/how-to-survive/
how-to-survive-tips-tab-02.html

Expert Village Video Series: How to Survive in the
Desert www.expertvillage.com/video-series/1429_
survive-desert.htm

Lawrence of Arabia (PBS)
www.pbs.org/lawrenceofarabia

Maricopa County Dept. of Emergency Management
Desert Awareness Booklet
www.maricopa.gov/Emerg_Mgt/pdf/SURVIVAL.
PDF

U.S Army Field Manual 3-05.70: Survival (May, 2002)
www.equipped.com/fm3-0570.htm

Desert Preservation and Desertification

Biological Soil Crusts www.soilcrust.org

The Center for Sonoran Desert Studies of the Desert
Research Institute, NV www.dri.edu

Desertification http://desertification.wordpress.com

The International Center for Agricultural Research
in the Dry Areas www.icarda.org

The Jacob Blaustein Institutes for Desert Research,
Ben-Gurion University of the Negev, Israel
http://desert.bgu.ac.il

SciDevNet: Desert Science
www.scidev.net/en/agriculture-and-environment/
desert-science

United Nations Conference on Desertification
www.unccd.int

United Nations World Food Program
www.wfp.org

General

Google Maps http://maps.google.com/maps

National Oceanic & Atmospheric Administration
www.noaa.gov

National Park Service www.nps.gov

Sacred Destinations
www.sacred-destinations.com

United Nations Educational, Scientific and Cultural
Organization World Heritage Convention
http://whc.unesco.org

United States Department of the Interior Bureau
of Land Management www.blm.gov

United States Fish and Wildlife Service
www.fws.gov

United States Geological Survey
www.usgs.gov

Index